Writers of Wales

Editors
MEIC STEPHENS   R. BRINLEY JONES

James A. Davies

LESLIE
NORRIS

University of Wales Press

Cardiff 1991

I

During the 1930s, on his way home from Cyfarthfa Castle Grammar School, the young Leslie Norris often loitered in the Merthyr branch of W.H. Smith. Under the benevolently blind eye of the staff he dipped frequently into the new poetry books; during one period he even read his way through twenty-five volumes of Doughty's ARABIA DESERTA. He could rarely afford to buy, though he once saved up for Edward Thomas's THE TRUMPET AND OTHER POEMS, *the first book of individual poetry I had ever owned.*

Norris has written of these book-shop experiences on more than one occasion. Across a lifetime they remain important to him. They are important to us for two reasons. First, in this memory of a solitary boy browsing eagerly is a reminder of how isolated he has often been from the Welsh literary world, particularly during his formative years. Though he began writing poetry when he was seven and though fine teachers fostered his enthusiasm, at least until the appearance of his pamphlet, TONGUE OF BEAUTY (1943), he knew no poets let alone a literary world. WALES and THE WELSH REVIEW seem never to have been on sale in Merthyr; he first heard of them long after they had folded. Leslie Norris has never wholly lost this 'outsider' status — his 'exile' in England and the USA has ensured that — though 'outsider' can seem an odd term for so sociable a man.

2   Secondly, in looking out of the everyday life of between-wars Merthyr into that literary world made manifest and compellingly glamorous in slim volumes from London publishers, Norris enacted, we see with hindsight, what has become his characteristic stance. For he explores, repeatedly, alternative areas of experience to the present, to the routine, to the superficially civilized, alternatives that include the past, or the unexpected, or the natural world that can reassure but often disturbs. Such areas lie close to the ordinary and are often entered suddenly. In this sense, 'otherness' is his main concern. As he puts it in 'Finding Gold': *one step from broken practice the spread gold lies.*

The line is a suitable epigraph for both life and work. The boy who stepped out of Merthyr's drab High Street into poetry and the deserts of Arabia became the man who left a steady job in Merthyr for a Midlands teacher-training college and schools in Somerset and Sussex, meanwhile establishing himself as a poet in England, *writing alone and . . . who looked almost entirely to London,* then left his highly successful career in education to become, in 1973, aged fifty-two, a full-time writer. Ten years later, when most think of retiring, after numerous visits to the USA he began an association with Brigham Young University in Utah. He is now Humanities Professor of Creative Writing in its Department of English. In 1989 he cut his last physical ties with Wales when he sold his cottage at Saron in Dyfed, which he had owned and used since the 1950s. He now divides most of his year between Utah and his British home near Chichester.

Norris's has been, continues to be, a life of *broken*

practice. He has never lacked the courage to sample alternatives; he has never lost the eagerness to explore of that boy in Smith's. And thus he has become an exile who looks back less and less at what he left and lost, and turns more and more to new worlds and experiences. This has made for a complex relationship with his native country.

On the one hand is an essentially Celtic attitude to the creative process at work on material that is often, of course, in itself Welsh. Though he believes that *I do not know when I begin what is going to happen in my stories. I am as surprised as any reader . . . I'm right up there, listening, even to the whispers,* and, *when the poem comes along I try to be ready for it. In training, my ears and eyes alert,* the imagery — of eavesdropping, so often the outsider's stance, and sport—deconstructs any tendency towards a sense of mystical inspiration. Rather, the stress is on subjecting ideas to obsessive craftsmanship: *And afterwards, I am the fellow who cuts the story to size;* he is *content to be at work to make [the poem] as complete as my ability will allow, cutting . . . and refining.* In his repeated emphasis on the *craft* of writing Norris echoes ancient bardic traditions within which the poet is no languid romantic waiting for a fully-fledged poem or story to arrive by divine messenger but an alert man with practised literary techniques whose ideas are cherished and shaped, this last often slowly and painfully, into acceptable public statements. Norris shares with Dylan Thomas, the greatest of modern Welsh literary 'makers', the perfectionist's desire to apply craft to sullen art.

On the other hand, his relations with the Welsh literary establishment have often been uneasy, his

4 allegiance seemingly elsewhere. In 1970, when a POETRY WALES editorial argued that Welsh writers should publish in Wales, he defended himself vigorously by insisting that no Welsh publisher, at that time, had the editorial expertise, feeling for his work and commercial advantages of Chatto & Windus. Further, after the success of FINDING GOLD and with RANSOMS about to appear, Wales could seem a limiting place. In 1969 he attended a launch in Swansea of the important Anglo-Welsh anthology, THE LILTING HOUSE, and wrote to William Plomer: *whenever I go to Wales to such a gathering I am more aware of how* unlike *the Welsh poets I am. I have little real sympathy with such parochialism.*

His career has been punctuated by provocative gestures. In 1967, with other Welsh writers he signed Harri Webb's petition in support of the 'Welsh Rule' at the National Eisteddfod but made it plain to Webb that he did so to oppose poetry competitions in English, a likely consequence, Norris considered, of that rule being rescinded. Three years later 'A Small War' was rejected by POETRY WALES.

This powerful poem, with its superb opening description of the young Norris cycling over the Beacons to his cousin's farm in a Senni Valley that, in the late 1960s, was threatened with flooding for a reservoir, has controversial closing stanzas:

> *I would not fight for Wales, the great battle-cries*
> *Do not arouse me. I keep short boundaries holy,*
> *Those my eyes have recognised and my heart has known*
> *As welcome. Nor would I fight for her language . . .*
> *It's the small wars I understand . . .*

I will not argue with, and the slow cattle swinging
    weightily
Home. When I open the taps in my English bathroom
I am surprised they do not run with Breconshire blood.

I think it's typical of the attitude of most Welshmen:
we'd fight happily and bitterly for our own bro, but
for little else, Norris wrote in his covering letter. A
second letter stressed ironic elements in the
poem. But Meic Stephens, then editor of POETRY
WALES, though Norris's friend, felt such
sentiments to be unacceptable, a response that
disturbed and saddened the author but did not
change his views. The poem was later published
in THE ANGLO-WELSH REVIEW and collected in
MOUNTAINS POLECATS PHEASANTS (1974). In 1972
Norris again stood out against prevailing Welsh
literary opinion with a letter to POETRY WALES
fiercely attacking R.S. Thomas's poetry for its
restricted vision of Wales and lack of *human*
generosity and tenderness evident in his treatment
of Iago Prytherch.

Such distancing gestures are manifestations of
Norris's complex sense of his own poetic identity.
In 1967, writing to Meic Stephens about Martin
Corner's review of FINDING GOLD in POETRY WALES,
he regretted that an English reviewer had been
chosen:

We write in a small idiom & for a few people. We do not
really write in English at all, nor from an English tradition,
& a critic of our poetry needs new terms & tools for
evaluating it. . . . No, English yardsticks are not for us.

6   Three years later he wrote again to Meic
    Stephens:

*although I live in England and my subject matter is less
specifically Welsh than that of my friends, there are ways,
traditional ways of thinking and concerns of texture and
technique, in which I am the most Welsh of all contem-
porary Anglo-Welsh poets, and that I feel myself most
strongly allied to Welsh writers, even those who write in
Welsh.*

Yet, at about the same time he insisted, in a letter
to Sam Adams about Anglo-Welshness: *I don't
believe it exists. I see myself as an English poet,
writing in English.* His Welshness, he considered,
stemmed from the occasional *use of a Welsh
landscape & images* and, crucially, from the fact
that *up to 17 or 18 years, will see the formation of
nearly all a poet's* basic *imagery.*

Here are the tensions of exile but the contradiction
is more apparent than real. Norris regards himself
as a Welsh poet, as the product of a Welsh
upbringing and drawing on aspects of the Welsh
literary tradition. None the less, he sees himself as
part of the unique Welsh element of the wider
English tradition. Any attempt to assess him must
take account, it seems, of both Welsh and English
elements. In this sense he cannot be regarded,
simply, as writing *from an English tradition* (the
second, understood, 'really' in that first quotation
— *nor [really] from an English tradition* — makes the
necessary subtle distinction).

Until comparatively recently, his work has been
more warmly recognized outside Wales. His

compatriots have often been wary of him, as the
response to 'A Small War' makes clear. Years after
Meic Stephens's initial misgivings, Tony Conran,
reviewing SELECTED POEMS in PLANET, commented on
the poem's closing lines: *Come off it, who do you think
you're kidding? . . . Like any middlebrow Englishman,
emotionally, he eats his cake and has it too*, though in
writing this Conran missed the self-deprecating,
perhaps rather English *surprised* in the poem's final
line. More generally, Mike Jenkins has noted the
scant social and political awareness in the work of
a writer brought up in between-wars Merthyr,
Randal Jenkins his failure to analyse and explain
the experiences here re-creates. Others, notably Gillian
Clarke and Robert Nisbet, have complained of a
digressive approach and a decorative use of
language. To Robert Minhinnick this is *needless and
inappropriate overwriting*. The Welsh literary world
has found it hard not to be critical.

Norris's literary career was London-based and is
now American-orientated. His work is invariably
first published in the USA and increasingly reflects
his American experiences. There he is much in
demand as writer, reader and teacher of creative
writing. His work is widely and favourably noticed.
That said, some American reviewers sound a
puzzled note that can echo those far-off Welsh
reservations. Reactions to THE GIRL FROM CARDIGAN
make this point: at least three major literary pages
— those in the NEW YORK TIMES BOOK REVIEW, the
HOUSTON POST and the LOS ANGELES TIMES — in
generally glowing reviews find an old-fashioned
quality in work that is very different from most
modern, franker, more brutal fiction. Behind such
comments is a shared sense of significant omissions

from Norris's work: there is little on politics or social concerns, and comparatively little on relations between adults, particularly those involving sex, love and marriage.

Leslie Norris's concerns are determinedly elsewhere: he is so often a nature poet, and a writer about childhood. He is, ostensibly at least, 'celebratory' to an extent unusual for his time. Yet those who criticize him for omissions and seeming evasions, or who regard him as no more than a misplaced Georgian, miss the distinct and disconcerting modernity of his work. He is a special kind of outsider, a poetic borderer. His nature poetry, for example, so often presses against atavistic frontiers, closer to Ted Hughes than, say, to W.H. Davies. His best work, poetry and prose, is sad, tense, and gesturing towards the fragmentary, often with a disturbing open-endedness that has been much misunderstood. Rather than re-assuringly remaking the world it discomfortingly deconstructs it.

II

Leslie Norris's paternal grandfather was from Slough. Norris's mother's family originally came from near Cynghordy in Dyfed and were in Merthyr before 1881, drawn from their rural world to that booming centre of industry as part of the great nineteenth-century internal migration. In a manner that prefigured their descendant's habitual literary stance they did not so much move from one world to another as settle at the border of the new: the Joneses rented a farm above the smoky town and Leslie Norris's great-grandfather, *obscure & dying young*, bred and reared ponies for the coal-mines.

The farm was Y Wern, oak-beamed in its oldest part, on the mountain between Merthyr and Aberdare, where Norris's grandfather, Daniel Owen Jones, was born. It was later farmed by John Jones, Daniel's elder brother who, like his father before him, was also a bailiff for the Cyfarthfa Estate. Dan Jones was articled to a fitter in Cyfarthfa Works, married a Merthyr woman and set up home at 9 Cyfarthfa Row. He was a cultured man who wrote verse in Welsh and was a deacon at Bethel Welsh Baptist Chapel in Merthyr's Georgetown district. Norris's father, George William Norris, was born in Cardiff and moved to Merthyr when still a boy. He was one of a large family. Some of his brothers and sisters left for west Wales, to Lower Cwmtwrch and villages in north Carmarthenshire. Others farmed in the Senni Valley near Brecon. George

Norris stayed, working first as a miner, then, after the First World War, when his health declined, as a milkman. He married Dan Jones's daughter, Mary Jane, and moved into 11 Hankey Terrace on Merthyr's south side. In this small terraced house, on 21 May 1921, George Leslie Norris was born.

In the Merthyr of his childhood were lingering remains of the old rumbustious town of Glyn Jones and Jack Jones. A Spanish area and an Irish one recalled the times when the ironworks at Cyfarthfa and Dowlais were the greatest in Europe and a magnet for workers. By 1921 such days had gone; indeed, in that year 3,000 Dowlais steelworkers were made redundant, marking the end of Merthyr's industrial buoyancy and signalling the slide into dreadful economic depression. During the 1920s 1,000 people each year left the borough in search of work; by 1939 over 25,000 had gone for good. In 1936 over 60 per cent of those who remained were unemployed, rising to almost 70 per cent in 1939. Many houses were unfit for human habitation; malnutrition and the diseases of poverty, including tuberculosis, were rife; children went barefoot to school. In 1939 the planning organization, Political and Economic Planning, considered Merthyr to be beyond economic redemption. It proposed closing down the town and rebuilding it on the banks of the Usk in rural Gwent.

Leslie Norris grew up in depressed Merthyr as the eldest of three brothers, the other two, Eric and Gordon, being born, in 1924 and 1926 respectively, in Garden Street, a poorer street than Hankey Terrace and near the River Taff. Gordon became a headteacher in England; Eric spent his working life

in the garage business in Merthyr. At various times
as the family's fortunes fluctuated they also lived in
Seward Street, Mardy Terrace and Solomon Street,
Penydarren. But his memories of childhood are not
much preoccupied with economic and social
deprivation. They are mainly a series of glowing
and positive pictures.

Norris's home was a happy one; his father loved
animals, made furniture, read avidly and, when
the moment was right, was *a superb raconteur and
storyteller*, with a talent for reciting humorous
verse. On many evenings, when he had eaten and
read he would entertain his boys with his day's
adventures on the milk-round: *The stories were so
well told that they happened in a world as real to us as the
one in which our own house stood.* He was also a good
singer but would only perform when the children
were ill. His mother could speak Welsh but English
was the language of the home and the street.

For the young Leslie, as the Norris family moved
around Merthyr, Y Wern Farm was a constant. He
spent much of his time on the borders of industrial
Merthyr in that farmhouse full of talk, people and,
in particular, story-telling that aroused the
imagination so that *I ran shivering through the shadows
for my own house in the town.* There, too, he developed
the love of nature and animals inherited from his
father.

From 1926 to 1931 Norris attended Georgetown
Primary School. This was a time of dreadful poverty:
in a class that was never less than forty he was the
only boy with shoes. But, for four years, he was
taught by *a great genius* named Brinley Phillips,

affectionately described many years later:

I know exactly where I was when I first heard that Pwyll prince of Dyved was minded to go hunting in Glyn Cuch. With more than forty other small boys I was sitting in a class-room in Georgetown School, Merthyr Tydfil. The afternoon was cold and dark, and our teacher had put a match to the frail, incandescent globes of the gaslight. High above our heads the small flames bubbled and popped, the weak light not enough to drive the shadows from the corners of the room. Our teacher stood directly beneath them, so that he could see better. He wore pince-nez, with a thin chain hanging from them, although he was a young man and a good footballer. Opening [THE MABINOGION], he began to read the story of the prince who went willingly down into hell for a year, and just as willingly we went with him, knowing that in the world of stories all would be well and that we should return in time to run home through the bitter weather.

Brinley Phillips was a profound influence on the young Norris. He introduced the boy to a wide range of imaginative literature; Norris still recalls *the sensitivity of his attitude to words*. Further, he educated his charges into a precise awareness of the world. As Norris puts it: *What he did was educate our senses.*

Phillips's former pupils still remember the originality of his teaching methods. He once gave each pupil a piece of card in the centre of which was a small hole through which each had to look intently at a small framed part of their surroundings, thus developing their powers of detailed observation of a world made new and strange through concentration. The activity now seems a paradigm for Norris's subsequent literary

career. On one stormy day Phillips took his class to
the large trees in the school yard and made each
pupil put an ear to the bark and arms around the
trunk. As the wind blew each *heard the tree protesting*
and felt its mysterious life. Many years later, when
Norris wrote

> *the creaking fibres*
> *Of oak and hanging beech*

to end the first stanza of 'Travelling West', he
was remembering that childhood moment long
ago in Wales as he did, even later, in parts of the
sequence 'Stones Trees Water'. It comes as no
surprise that Norris began writing poems as
early as Standard I. The influence of that dead
teacher lives on in his former pupil's closely
observed imaginative responses to nature and is
another reason why a celebratory, at times
idyllic, treatment of childhood has come easily to
him.

In 1931 Norris passed the scholarship examination
for Cyfarthfa Castle Grammar School and, that
autumn, began the daily walk to school through
the ruins of the old Cyfarthfa works. His English
teacher, Sam Adams, had once taught Glyn Jones,
who described him as *an elegant and formidable mid-
get, remembered by Leslie as a fine teacher of literature.*
Norris continued to write; once a year he and a few
friends contributed verse to a newspaper produced
in aid of the local hospital. He entered the literary
competitions in school eisteddfods. But, generally,
in the manner of the time, his school did not
encourage much extra-curricular literary activity. *I
wrote a lot of verse there,* Norris once wrote of his

days at the Castle, *but nobody seemed to care very much*. During this period he browsed in the High Street bookshop, discovering Hopkins and, momentously, Dylan Thomas: he read 'The force that through the green fuse' in BEST POEMS OF 1934 *and for the first time saw what poetry could really do.*

He was a popular boy, a good runner who, eventually, played on the wing for the school's First XV, a keen boxer and, in particular, a fine footballer who had played for Georgetown School and then in the Merthyr League. These sporting interests, plus passions for fishing and horses, have stayed with him throughout his life. His talent for limericks, parodies and squibs about teachers amused his friends. But he was also a serious boy who left Bethel Welsh Baptist chapel for Market Square English Presbyterian Church so that he could understand the services. Occasionally he accompanied Roman Catholic cousins to their church on Brecon Road because, as he puts it: *I loved the ritual and came to appreciate the symbolism.*

All these interests have found their way into his writing. Above all, his time at Y Wern, together with holidays on farms owned by his relatives in west Wales, further deepened the love of the natural world that, even in Merthyr's ruined valley, was never far away. What he wrote of Glyn Jones's Merthyr still applied to his own:

A boy living in that place, particularly a boy who is to be a poet, could see with delight the solitary birds and animals of the inhospitable hills, curlew, fox, ring-ousel, and twenty minutes later be scuffling with his friends in the High Street.

For close at hand and often visited was that other beguiling and spectacularly beautiful world of what was to become the Brecon Beacons National Park.

Norris published his first poem in 1938. He was then seventeen. During that same year he left school. Brinley Phillips had followed his grammar-school career and was to take a friendly interest in his literary progress. But despite Phillips's encouragement higher education was financially impossible. So he began work as a rates clerk in Merthyr Town Hall. In his spare time he studied accountancy, though *sporadically & to no avail*. Two years later, in May 1940, he was called up. He trained as an airframe fitter in the RAF at Blackpool and Little Rissington, only to contract severe blood-poisoning from handling steel ropes. In June 1941, gravely ill, he was invalided out. This was an unhappy, troubled time: the war raged on, taking away most and claiming several of his Merthyr friends, his convalescence lasted for months, his father was suffering from cancer and died in 1942. Eventually he returned to the town hall and worked out the rest of the war in *uncongenial employment*.

Sport helped sustain him; when an injury curtailed his soccer he became a referee and an organizer of Merthyr Referees Society. He read voraciously, admiring Defoe, who, he noted, *makes us believe*, Hemingway, Dashiell Hammett, Caradoc Evans and other Anglo-Welsh writers of the day. These included Glyn Jones: *you can't imagine the number of times I read his 'The Blue Bed' & 'The Water Music', I cut my poetic teeth . . . on his works*. Above all, he continued to write poetry, the strained desperation of which reflected his feelings during this time.

Towards the middle of the Second World War Norris replied to what he considered to be an ill-informed letter to a newspaper about *the nature of creative writing*. The letter-writer was Peter Baker, who wrote to Norris offering to publish his work. They met in London and Norris, in his early twenties, found his publisher to be even younger. Baker's 'The Favil Press', later 'Falcon Press', and first based in Kensington High Street, published a series of pamphlets, called 'Resurgam Younger Poets', that included early work by Paul Scott and Alex Comfort. Norris's TONGUE OF BEAUTY (1943) was the ninth. Unusually and, in the chaos of wartime London, probably mistakenly, it was reviewed in two consecutive issues of THE TIMES LITERARY SUPPLEMENT, both reviewers praising 'Poem in Ten Parts', a religious sequence comprising half the pamphlet. Otherwise it attracted little interest. Three years later the contents of TONGUE OF BEAUTY were reprinted as part of POEMS (1946), also published by Peter Baker. This attracted even less attention.

The door that had suddenly opened at least on to the fringes of the London literary world quickly closed. Back in Merthyr Norris worked on. But after the war the town changed profoundly. In the comparative prosperity of the late 1940s and early 1950s coal-pits began to close and lighter industries replaced the old steelworks. Slum-clearance and improvements swept away much of old Merthyr, including the riverside area with Garden Street and the adjacent urban sprawl that once constituted the notorious 'China' and 'Arches' areas made famous in Jack Jones's novels. Much of old Georgetown, including its school, disappeared under new housing estates. Y Wern Farm lost its fields and its pond, the scene of 'Dead Boys', to a rugby club. The Joneses had left the farm for Cyfarthfa Row, which, in its turn, was demolished. Many of Norris's friends had died in the war. The intelligent young, supported by State grants, left the old and declining valley town for universities and colleges and lives elsewhere. In 1948 Leslie Norris, aged twenty-seven, a rates clerk in Merthyr Town Hall, doubtless felt the surge of the times and the call of the new as his ancestors had, years ago, when industrial Merthyr had beckoned the rural poor. It was time to go.

On 31 July 1948 he married Catherine ('Kitty') Morgan, of Balaclava Road, Dowlais. It was her second marriage. She had trained as a chemist but marriage had made her a housewife. Weeks later Norris became a student at City of Coventry Teacher Training College and has never since lived permanently in Wales.

For, after college, he became an English teacher in Grass Royal School, Yeovil, Somerset, moving in 1952 to Southdown Junior School in Bath where he was deputy head. He then became headteacher of Westergate School, Chichester, West Sussex, he and Kitty settling in nearby Aldingbourne. Near-neighbours have included the poets Andrew Young and Ted Walker, the Norris's friendship with and kindness towards the former lightening the years before his death in 1971. From 1955 to 1958 he wrote an M.Phil. thesis on Vernon Watkins at Southampton University and, in 1958, obtained a lectureship at Bognor Regis College of Education, later West Sussex Institute of Higher Education, where, from 1966, his wife also taught.

In a decade *caught up in a career in education* Norris had achieved much. He settled into the busy life of a college lecturer. From time to time he published poems in, for example, THE LONDON MAGAZINE, THE LISTENER and POETRY REVIEW. In 1964, encouraged by Richard Church, he made a selection from his work, called it DEAD BOYS, and began approaching publishers. In 1966, with Church as intermediary, Cecil Day-Lewis, of Chatto & Windus/The Hogarth Press, expressed interest. A much-changed selection, with a new poem, 'Finding Gold', strengthening the volume and supplying its superb title, was published in 1967 in the distinguished 'Phoenix Living Poets' series that included work by Norman MacCaig, D.J. Enright, James Merrill, Laurie Lee, John Fuller and Jon Silkin. During the previous year he had made his first significant contact with the Anglo-Welsh literary world: he gave his first reading in Wales, met Glyn Jones and became a founder member of the Guild of Welsh Writers. In 1967 ten 'Merthyr' poems later to be included in FINDING GOLD were published by Meic Stephens as a 'Triskel Poets' pamphlet entitled THE LOUD WINTER.

At the age of forty-six Norris had the beginnings of a reputation; it was consolidated up to 1980 by numerous readings and broadcasts and by three further volumes in the 'Phoenix Living Poets' series. FINDING GOLD was reprinted; RANSOMS won the Poetry Society's Alice Hunt Bartlett Prize for 1970. He was awarded a Cholmondeley Prize for poetry in 1978. His work continued to be sought after by anthologizers: by 1967 'The Ballad of Billy Rose', for example, had appeared in more than eighty places. He edited and contributed to Faber's memorial volume for Vernon Watkins. John Ormond filmed him at his cottage in Saron for BBC TV.

His poetry was becoming increasingly well known in the USA. Much of his finest work in RANSOMS, including 'Early Frost', 'Winter Song', 'Drummer Evans' and 'Water', first appeared in THE ATLANTIC MONTHLY. Others were taken by THE NEW YORKER. In the late 1960s an American agent asked him for fiction. Norris recalls: *I had not written any prose, not fiction. Contrite, I wrote a very short piece called 'Plus Fours', an example, I said, of my work. He sold it to THE ATLANTIC MONTHLY. I was away.* He was soon in demand. As a result of publishing short stories, *I keep getting letters from American publishers wanting a novel. I shan't write one, because I don't have that sort of mind, but it's flattering.*

Now in his late forties, he found it more and more difficult to combine his career in education — he had become a Principal Lecturer in Degree Studies at West Sussex Institute — with the increasing demands of his writing career. As early as 1967 he was *trying very hard to earn enough to give up teaching* and had a taste of full-time writing when an Arts Council award financed a year off in 1969. He used part of it to try longer fiction for children, though unsuccessfully. In the event America was the catalyst. In the summer of 1973 he accepted an invitation to be Visiting Professor and Poet at the University of Washington in Seattle. This he greatly enjoyed and the experience so unsettled him that, on his return, he resigned his lectureship to try to live by his pen.

At the age of fifty-two he stepped, characteristically, into a new and uncertain world. Norah Smallwood, his editor at Chatto & Windus, nervously reminded him that poems and short stories yielded only small financial returns. She need not have worried. Norris was in demand not only for his poetry and fiction but as a reader, broadcaster and reviewer. Further, he based his literary career on a foundation of awards and, particularly, visiting appointments. In 1974 the Arts Council made him a substantial grant; he was Resident Poet at Eton during 1977, held visiting appointments at Aston University and returned to West Sussex Institute in 1979-80 as Arts Council Writing Fellow.

He made further visits to the USA. In 1976 he and his wife had *a glorious time* on *a tiny island off the coast of Maine, from which I got a long poem I'm pleased with, then Boston, fêted and feasted, and again in New York.* The poem was the sequence ISLANDS OFF MAINE, the fêting and feasting marked Scribner's publication of SLIDING, the British edition of which won the 1978 David Higham Prize for Fiction. Also in 1978 New York's Viking Press published MERLIN AND THE SNAKE'S EGG, a volume of poetry for children.

Norris went back to Seattle in 1980 and 1981 and to East Carolina in 1982; he visited and read widely. In 1983 Brigham Young University, the Mormon foundation in Provo, Utah, invited him to be Visiting Poet. Thus began another important and continuing phase in Norris's life. He returned to Brigham

Young in 1984 and 1985, became Christiansen Professor of Poetry and Head of the Creative Writing Section of the Department of English and, in 1989, Humanities Professor of Creative Writing, teaching nineteenth- and twentieth-century poetry and an acclaimed course in creative writing.

His wife also teaches at Brigham Young and they now live in Utah for much of the year. For a one-time Merthyr Nonconformist this was certainly a step into an alien world, though Norris has never been afraid of that. He found himself to be at home in Mormon Utah and the Mormons *very strange and nice*. They were also tolerant: though teetotal themselves, *they don't seem to mind that I sneak into the State Liquor Store from time to time.* He remains attracted by the rituals of their churches, *but know I could not belong to them.* Further, *it is not a mystery that I should like Utah which has mountains, rivers, lakes, tips . . .,* just like Merthyr.

Despite the reservations of some he has become a senior figure amongst Welsh writers. Poems, short stories, the occasional article or review, still appear in Welsh literary magazines. The fortunate can sometimes hear him read. He has become well known as a translator of Welsh-language poetry, notably of Dafydd ap Gwilym and Gwenallt Jones. With the Germanist Alan Keele, he has begun publishing translations of Rilke. The Welsh Arts Council has awarded him prizes, notably in 1988 for THE GIRL FROM CARDIGAN, his second volume of short stories. He has become a Fellow of the Welsh Academy. He has adjudicated Welsh literary competitions, such as that for poetry at the Cardiff Literature Festival, and has left Chatto & Windus for the Bridgend-based publishers, Seren Books.

And yet, ironically, all this has occurred as physical exile in Utah or Aldingbourne has become more absolute. In his — and not only his — sense of the term he remains a Welsh writer but he is also, now, an established American academic. It is not surprising that he cherishes his American links given his high USA reputation. Peter Davison, the distinguished American poet and editor, once described Norris as the finest contemporary British poet; James Dickey once observed that the voice in Norris's poetry is one of the most authentic of contemporary writers. To return yet again to the reception of THE GIRL FROM CARDIGAN: it has been widely and enthusiastically reviewed in North America, in notices that often praise Norris's craftsmanship and power. The NEW YORK TIMES BOOK REVIEW stressed *the appeal — even the gravity — of naturalness and moments of freshness and power.* The LOS ANGELES TIMES found the stories *so distinct and fully realized that they have the resonance of novels.* The book has sold well in the USA, whereas in Britain as a whole it has attracted comparatively little attention.

Indeed, despite the prizes and the added recognition of becoming a Fellow of the Royal Society of Literature, Norris's work has drawn a varied response from British critics. Though, occasionally, a reviewer such as Richard Church, writing of FINDING GOLD in COUNTRY LIFE, has praised Norris's *tense awareness of the drama of living* and his *authoritative touch of simplicity*, other reviewers, English as well as Welsh, have found his work difficult to come to terms with. One or two have

fallen back on superficial criticism, or the
maliciousness that can proceed from a failure to
understand. Thus the anonymous reviewer of
FINDING GOLD in THE TIMES LITERARY SUPPLEMENT
found some *slack and sentimental* writing, with
a rather manufactured moral occasionally tacked on;
THE TABLET'S review of RANSOMS — *a couple of dozen
limp lyrics, or strained statements* — falls nastily into
the latter category. Perhaps significantly, more
distinguished reviewers have sensed the in-
adequacy of such responses: the slightly puzzled
reaction of some American reviewers to THE GIRL
FROM CARDIGAN — the contrasts, already noted,
with other modern writers of fiction — may well
have affinities with what, for example, Norman
Nicholson wrote of RANSOMS in the CHURCH TIMES:
*There is always a danger that such verse will seem
simpler, more open-handed than it really is,* a com-
ment close to that of Edward Lucie-Smith in his
observation in SOUTHERN ARTS that, in MOUNTAINS
POLECATS PHEASANTS, Norris's poems could seem
simple *at first.*

Norris's view of his own work emerges in an attempt
to account for his American popularity. It is, he
considers,

*because of the accessibility of my work, because of the colour
of my images, maybe the hint of an accent they like, because
I am a singer at a time when most Americans are speakers,
because I am neither timid nor wild, but quiet and
confident, because I work hard and it rarely shows, because
(in very small modest letters) I'm a bloody good writer.*

In congenial exile, rejecting self-indulgent *hiraeth*
and facile, distanced nationalism, Leslie Norris
turns eagerly, as he has always done, to the new

24   experiences that press upon him. His attempt to explain that American popularity ends at the point reached by a few of his reviewers and many of his general readers. To put this another way: he and those readers stand at the edge of the familiar and the understood. What lies beyond has never been adequately explained and assessed.

III

Leslie Norris has made two selections from his poetry: WALKING THE WHITE FIELDS (1980) and SELECTED POEMS (1986). Neither includes a poem from his first two publications, the pamphlet TONGUE OF BEAUTY (1943) and POEMS (1946). These volumes, now almost impossible to obtain, have become a forgotten false start, seemingly almost unconnected with the later part of his literary career.

There is good reason for this: its few readers agree that the early poetry is hardly accomplished and only occasionally promising. Sam Adams found *some extravagant writing and rather self-conscious posturing*; Randal Jenkins felt the poems expressed adolescent excess and overblown romanticism; Mercer Simpson considered them *self-indulgent emotionally, clouded with abstractions, and inconsistent in their grasp of form*. It is difficult to disagree; such titles as 'Dirge', 'Ashes to Ashes, Dust to Dust', or 'The Groping Heart', let alone lines like

> *I catch the night's sigh and cage it in my mind's bottle,*

or

> *I flame, a dragon's sigh through tooth-gapped air,*

meaning, 'I exhale in cold weather', are on the silly side of pretentious.

26   There is some late-adolescent love-poetry, such as 'Thinking of Winter', when the poet, *Devil or saint*, is

> *. . . caught in the net that your fingers*
> *Have made, my dear,*
> *And the tides of your murderous hair.*

There is an interesting, though mawkishly pretentious, poem on the death of Alun Lewis. But both volumes are dominated by two themes. The first is Norris himself, regarded with neurotic self-consciousness in 'I fear a grief' —

> *I fear a grief, that, like an unwilling thief steals*
> *Over-cautiously into my room today*

— and at length in 'Speaking to Friends'. This last is a four-part sequence in which Norris uses local topography — ruined urban Merthyr, the mountain road to Tredegar — to explore what for him was a time of frustration:

> *. . . the future comes upon you*
> *With a million todays, and your ambition*
> *Put in a pond in a sack*
> *Tied and stoned by circumstance.*

Above all, he is romantically aware of himself as poet, as in his title-poem:

> *I am the tongue of beauty, and I cry*
> *War to her enemies . . .*

Again, in 'Dirge',

My fingers are five birds, whose single songs
    Shall roost and flutter on the cloudy banks.

Of course these lines are pretentious, but they are interesting in identifying future concerns with beauty and nature that are further stressed when, in 'Sonnet for Myself', he asserts that *There grows a wood of words over my heart*. Even more prophetic, we now see, are lines from 'Song':

. . . I pick fastidiously, with a gloved hand, into the
Packed rag-bag of inspiration, ignoring with singular
Fortitude the more noisy aspirations of social and political
Implications. I choose old-fashioned words and subjects
Smooth-worn with time.

The other central subject is religion. *On what shore shall I be, bruised, cast*, he asks, with syntactical force, in 'Ashes to Ashes, Dust to Dust', a poem that seems, at least in part, a response to his father's death. Elsewhere is celebration, as in 'In Praise' (*Great great great is your glory*) and in 'On Hearing Debussy's Sunken Cathedral' (*Proud carillon, O shade of praise to God!*). Most important of all is 'Poem in Ten Parts', the sequence that dominates TONGUE OF BEAUTY. These mainly unrhymed and irregular sonnets respond to the Christian story from cosmic creation to Christ's death:

I feel a thorn inside the drop of tears;
I feel a spear stab bloodless to my side.
This was a saviour tortured to a tree.

They end with a pious appeal:

> ... *Storm*
> *Of my say, now blow the bitter Word*
> *To all earth's reaches, stamp the sullen Covenant*
> *On each man's heart, cable rich thought, or, knowing*
> *This world of need, uncross the bloody Christ.*

Inevitably, the juvenilia is rich evidence of unassimilated reading. There are echoes of Milton in *And hurled, half-clothed in light, to spin/ Through space*; Herbert stands squarely behind 'The Passion, Easter, 1944'; in 'Poem in Ten Parts — X' the phrase *cable rich thought* recalls 'The Collar'. In 'Two Songs' —

> *O, like the worm that sits inside the rose,*
> *I'll fellow Death*

— or, in 'Conversation' —

> *Then Death and the sisters Grief and Pollution*
> *came over the hill like a cloud*

— we hear William Blake. Yeatsian echoes include, in 'Sonnet in Winter': *Sick in the dying light, a man of visions.* More blatantly, the liturgical allusions in 'Ashes to Ashes, Dust to Dust' (*O God have mercy upon us in the hour of misery./O God!/O God have mercy.*) point to the T.S. Eliot of 'Ash Wednesday'. The Eliot of 'Burnt Norton' appears in 'Speaking to Friends', in such lines as:

> *Quietly, open your lily-leaves,*
> *Quietly, modestly, gaze from this height. . .*

Over there, beyond the edge of the pool . . .
The laughter of hidden children . . .

The greatest influence is Dylan Thomas and a few examples must stand for many. Thus, *uncross the bloody Christ*, in 'Poem in Ten Parts — X' and

> *. . . A flowed and flooded tide*
> *Sailed up the fields of skulls and buried bones*
> *And laid her carried love of sand and gentle stones*

from 'Conversation', look back, the latter also rhythmically, to the Thomas of 'I see the boys of summer'. 'After the funeral' contributes to *hooded Wales* ('Poem in Ten Parts — I'); in 'Letter to J.P.', *the spelling, compelling, autumn . . . crossing shapes of skeletons of winter trees* and, in 'Sonnet to Myself', *the speechless blood/That, shuddering through its course*, reveal too close an encounter with 'Especially when the October wind'. Versions of Thomas's grandly oratorical, neo-bardic style, are found almost everywhere.

Leslie Norris's susceptibility to Dylan Thomas's determinedly poetic assertiveness is a reminder that the young Thomas had also been obsessed with himself, struggling with words in a provincial town that had swirled antagonistically or indifferently around him. The self-consciousness of 'The Orchards', with its autobiographical subtext, and of the equally self-regarding poem, 'Ears in the turrets hear', in which he dramatized himself as an *island bound/By a thin sea of flesh/And a bone coast* in a world in which *Hands grumble on the door*, and *Ships anchor off the bay*, reflected a mind, as he told Vernon Watkins, troubled by *living in your own private, four-walled world as exclusively as possible*.

Yet, Dylan Thomas grew up in a large and relatively prosperous town and with congenial friends — Daniel Jones and Vernon Watkins among them — who shared his cultural interests and ambitions. Leslie Norris, only seven years younger, alone in depressed Merthyr, was sustained by his own determination. The dedication of 'Poem in Ten Parts' to *Elvet* (Howell Elvet Lewis, 1860–1953), who wrote poetry in Welsh and hymns in Welsh and in English, and who was Archdruid during the 1920s, but who has no obvious connection with Merthyr or with Norris, may be youthful pretension or a pious gesture, but may also indicate a deeper-seated longing for literary associations. Certainly, like Thomas, he shows a strong sense of his own uniqueness. And if, as seems appropriate, TONGUE OF BEAUTY and POEMS are compared to Thomas's famous notebooks, we see the most significant of all similarities: both poets, beginning, possessed immense emotional dynamism. Though Norris's juvenilia has occasional merit — there is some rhetorical power, an awareness of poetic form and some feeling for rhythm and line — it is, above all else, setting aside obvious weaknesses, moving evidence of the deep feelings, desperate longings, and intense empathetic gesturings of a young man bursting with undisciplined words and literary ambition. For him, like the young Dylan Thomas, *the future spread out beyond the window . . . and into smoky London paved with poems*. In Norris's own words, he wished to rise out of drab Merthyr *on a tower and wing of words/To the roof of the room of the world*.

As has been noted, Norris's concern with his own

writing afforded him glimmers of what might turn
out to be his future poetic course. With hindsight
we now recognize the prescience of lines from
'Men from the ends':

> *I know that beauty lives*
> *In memories that we have;*

and of the assertion in 'A Year to the Day':

> *Coming at last to the nearly remembered village,*
> *Close to the shore that I have only seen*
> *In dreams, the young man I had been*
> *Came out to meet me.*

He was slowly shifting from a concern with the
poetic and spiritual self to a response to different
areas of experience, in particular, to the
engagement with memory and the past that was
to fuel so much of his mature work. He was also
beginning to realize that this early voice was not
to be his own. Thus, in 'Song', in TONGUE OF
BEAUTY:

> *if, when I speak*
> *Of storm-clouds, I should say 'artillery of the skies',*
> *Just lean deeper*

> *Into your eminently luxurious cushions, and think it*
> *merely*
> *A sufficiently stirring simile.*

Again, in 'May Day', from POEMS:

> *The great sun — the magnificently reborn*

Emperor, the prince of immortal light,
I could say were this an epic poem.

In the love-poem, 'Thinking of Winter', he refers to a *secret . . . behind/ The bars and windows of your admired eyes*; but, he continues, *I dismiss the fancy as too poetic.*

The young Norris, impelled into poetry or, at least, poetic utterance, by the range and intensity of his feelings and unable as yet to find an appropriate language or sufficient poetic skill, is already demonstrating, wryly, the urge towards self-criticism, the ability to distance himself from his own writing, that distinguishes all writers of quality.

Twenty-one years later, 'More than Half Way There', the opening poem of FINDING GOLD and, as Norris's equivalent of 'Once it was the colour of saying', his final large gesture towards Dylan Thomas, is his last substantial comment on that early work. In 1967 Norris was forty-six, so that the title's sense of substantial achievement is deconstructed by a sadder sense of ageing. Stanza one looks back:

> *Obsessed by night, my young voice told*
> *Of swallows' ruby eyes between such trees*
> *As the cool moon allowed, and their dark*
> *Flight, elaborately simple, their desire*
> *Unthinkingly perfect, and their perfect songs.*

The juvenilia's undisciplined nature is skilfully suggested by the single sentence drifting away from its main verb and by the repetitive final line, its overwrought, idealized poetical world by

the jewelled language. Such memories menace
the maturing writer.

Yet, as stanza two asserts, *That was long ago*. Norris's
work has changed and so has the poem's style,
from the overly poetic to a simpler diction and to
speech-rhythms only slightly formalized:

> *I walk in the afternoons. The common*
> *Blackbird sings and I accept this marvel.*

He now writes of what he can see, of the marvels
of ordinary natural life. But the difference is not
absolute nor the feelings unambiguous. Though
he also insists, *I use my nights for twitching/Sleep
now*, the disturbed sleep and the pun on
twitching, a colloquialism for 'bird-watching',
creates a subtext suggestive of a troubled
subconscious still *obsessed by night*. Further, the
opening assertion (*That was long ago*) is both a
firm rejection of old ways and, in its cadence, an
expression of regret.

This tension between past and present ways of
writing is explored in the third and final stanza:

> *To protect any true voice, even one like this,*
> *Means constant vigilance. Each day I watch*
> *An older hand take the food to my mouth.*
> *I am alert lest an old voice soften*
> *What needs to be said. Guard. Silence if necessary.*

The stanza's anti-lyrical style, in part a
consequence of decreasing sentence length,
characterizes the *true voice* as one that speaks
directly of ordinary life. To *protect* it, to prevent

old ways returning too amply, is a constant struggle. The poem ends disturbingly, for at the stanza's centre are images of old age, helplessness and senility, that also imply reversion to poetic childhood.

The movement from past to present and to hints of a problematic future is also dramatized by the changing relationship between sentence and stanza. Initially the former is perfectly matched with the latter; stanza two has four sentences all working against the line; stanza three is staccato with five. Thus, as the poem proceeds it tends to fragment, generating an increasing tension between part and whole that exhibits the older poet's struggle to impose order on less tractable material.

'More than Half Way There' is a key poem in Norris's career because it describes the effects on his poetry of twenty-one years of hard work and changing perceptions from POEMS to FINDING GOLD. It is also important in that it illustrates two central characteristics of Norris's mature work: the built-in deconstructive tendency so often evident in the sadder subtext to seemingly celebratory or optimistic lines and, secondly, in the poem's contrast between present and past, the familiar and strange 'otherness', the juxtaposition of areas of experience that characterizes his work as well as his life.

FINDING GOLD, which includes most of THE LOUD WINTER, together with RANSOMS, MOUNTAINS POLECATS PHEASANTS and WATER VOICES, 106 poems in all, are the bedrock of Norris's poetic achievement. As the placing of 'More than Half Way There' makes clear, FINDING GOLD is the true beginning of his literary career. In this volume 'otherness' mainly means the past — more precisely, a lost Merthyr childhood. This last is explored in two poems — 'Dead Boys' and 'An Evening by the Lake' — placed, significantly, immediately after 'More than Half Way There'.

'Dead Boys' demonstrates the extent to which Norris had found his own voice. Here is artful discursiveness, a paring-down of previous prolixity, a new kind of writing:

> All night long, all one long winter night,
> The old tin Fords stood with their headlights turned
> On its drowning ice, thin as a ripped sheet,
> Where the covered slider lay in his silent bubbles
> And would not be found.

This is typical: the rhythms at once conversational and subtly heightened into suggestive cadences; lines that re-enact rather than simply describe, as in the opening dramatization of time passing slowly; the simple diction including the odd suggestive image, such as that of the ripped sheet, with its connotations of poverty and a covered body; the constant sense of a mind feeling its way into strange, far-off and sad territory. The rhetoric has gone, as has the overwriting. In its place, in a poem that recalls an incident from Norris's childhood when a friend died in a frozen pond, is a controlled account of one of Norris's central subjects:

> And the grown man smiles as returning he meets,
> In his eyed love, the cold, immortal children.
> They run unblighted the green lanes of their time.

'An Evening by the Lake' is also set in Merthyr. The narrator, revisiting Cyfarthfa School, watches boys playing near the lake and remembers an incident from his school-days when he and his friends took part in a boat race. 'Dead Boys' ends with poignant ambiguity:

Here, where the field was, they live, the dead boys.

This second poem has the same kind of conclusion in which assertion only generates uncertainty:

. . . All right, so my youth is dead,
And yes, those boys are gone.

For Norris's feelings about his childhood are very mixed. Though his children *run unblighted the green lanes of their time* in all their *bright innocence*, though he celebrates, in the rowing race, a moment of absorbed happiness and beauty, yet childhood was also an *angular* time of awkward, wrong, sad, tragic happenings. He writes of the boys playing by the lake:

these later voices,
And this younger water, which have
Entered the locked cellar of my mind,
Broken its seal, and let its darkness
Out.

This is both positive, shedding light on childhood, and negative, allowing the *darkness* of childhood to enter the adult present. Once again the deconstructive turn rejects simplifications.

The influence of Dylan Thomas has not wholly
disappeared from these poems. His cadences are
present, for example, in 'Dead Boys' in such lines as
The women sailed it/On gentle breath and *Nights buried
his foundered sadness in their tides*. But Norris's shift
to a more conversational style and his attitude to
the past now depends as much on Edward Thomas,
to whom he was later to pay his dues in 'Ransoms'
and 'A Glass Window', whose dark, troubled sense
of lost childhood in, say, 'Old Man' or 'The Path',
helps fill his successor's *locked cellar*. The shift
depends more on Wordsworth. In 'Dead Boys', *the
boy in his eyeless sight/Saw the face of the drowned*, recalls
the drowned man in THE PRELUDE, Book V, and the
reaction of young Wordsworth, whose *inner eye had
seen/Such sights before*; 'An Evening by the Lake'
looks to the rowing scene in Book I; 'A February
Morning', hearing *The voice of a singing woman ... /
Unhurried, passionate, clear, a voice of grief* draws on
'A Solitary Reaper'; much later, the famous short
story, 'Sliding', is another inter-textual reference,
this time to THE PRELUDE'S skating scene.

Such a conscious craftsman as Norris must surely
have been aware of these Wordsworthian
borrowings. Certainly their appearance is
significant. For the replacement of Dylan Thomas
by Wordsworth is important in two ways. Together
with the influence of Edward Thomas
Wordsworth's prominence marks the extent to
which Norris, whilst retaining Welsh connections,
had moved into the mainstream of English poetry.
Secondly, the shift from Dylan Thomas to
Wordsworth is from a major influence on style to
an influence on subject matter, in this case a
preoccupation with childhood, even though

Norris's response to this last is ambivalent, to say the least.

On the one hand, in 'Snow', a slight poem in which Norris, unusually, falls for *rainbow robins* clichés, adults behind windows, with eyes *Thirty years cleaner*, watch children *twirling the prodigal snow* and feel, again, the innocence of childhood. 'At Usk' describes a child in a graveyard *measuring with happy care . . . her offering/of snowdrop and crocus.* Young David Beynon, whose heroic death is celebrated in 'Elegy for David Beynon', even played rugby with concern, *careful/to miss us with your scattering/knees.* In 'A Small War' the young Norris is *a centaur-cyclist* pedalling out of Merthyr to *an Eden fourteen miles from home.* On 'Ravenna Bridge' a boy skips on the parapet and *kept for all himself/ The edges, even, of his happiness.* Childhood is a self-contained, caring, intense, instinctively happy world, summed up in 'The Old Age of Llywarch Hen' as

> *. . . the hospitable house of youth*
> *Where once I too had room and all the truth*
> *I wanted was in four small walls.*

Yet, such a summing-up demonstrates why Norris's best work rejects sentimentality. His positive statements are invariably qualified, as, here, in the suggestion that there are other, less desirable truths, and in the use of *small*.

'Water', set at Y Wern Farm, is a central and justly famous poem about remembering childhood. The adult narrator recalls staying, when a boy, at his aunt's farm and helping to provide drinks for children from the town who passed the farm on summer mornings and evenings on their way up and down the mountain. The poem divides into three parts. The first is stanza one:

> *On hot summer mornings my aunt set glasses*
> *On a low wall outside the farmhouse,*
> *With some jugs of cold water.*
> *I would sit in the dark hall, or*
> > *Behind the dairy window,*
> *Waiting for children to come from the town.*

Two factual, almost prosaic, sentences set the scene. In relating precisely to the lines and then the stanza, they create a first impression of order and control, which is quickly countered by the lack of rhyme and regularity, and by the slightly unexpected syntax, separating *glasses* and *jugs*, that hints at the effort to recollect. That effort is further stressed by the generalizing of the memory: the number of mornings, glasses, jugs and children are not specified; the low wall may be one of several; we remain slightly uncertain about where the boy waits, or how he waits in the dairy. And the tense of *I would sit* slides away from the definite 'I sat' into a mixture of insistence and desire that hazes further that seeming certainty.

The second part is stanzas two to five, describing the arrival of the children, their drinking, and the glimpsed ascent of the mountain. The part itself further divides into two: stanzas two, three and four, and stanza five. In the former, the children are described, initially, with precision and the simple past tense: *They came in small groups . . . they turned in at our gate.* At times firm stresses give them solidity: *They climbed with unsteady certainty.* But this is not sustained: momentary early definiteness and later solid stresses are, again, blurred when the tense changes: *They would stand . . . They would pass.* As for the boy: *would* on one occasion becomes *could.* And though *would* gives way, once, to the simple past — *I wondered what it was they knew the mountain had* — even here the boy's uncertainty counters precision. Indeed, the recollection becomes even more problematic through changes of person, the mingling of first-person singular and first-person plural. Lines and stanzas, the two main bases of order, are again subverted, this time by the superior power of sentence-enjambment. Consonantal language that resists lyrical flow (*They came in small groups, serious, steady . . . Their heads were a resolute darkness among ferns*), staccato punctuation, sentences that can close abruptly (*But they never looked at us.*), help dramatize this effort of recollecting what, in any case, is always slightly blurred.

Stanza five is different. It consists of a single sentence that, in shaping and being shaped by the stanza, reasserts order and aesthetic arrangement. And as the children climb the mountain the language changes:

> *Then it was open world, too high and clear*
> > *For clouds even, where over heather*
> *The free hare cleanly ran, and the summer sheep.*

The stresses have lightened, vowel effects increased, the movement has become more lyrical. These differences help set the stanza against its predecessors. So do further contrasts: the new freedom and openness with the indoors, hedged, walled world of the boy; the *free,* running natural world with the children who, regimented, *march up the soft, dirt road* and are then hemmed in by ferns. The children slide into indeterminacy as their tense changes to *They would pass.*

Thus, what might appear to be clear, detailed recollection is in reality uncertain, blurring, shifting, its several small transitions — from tense to tense, person to person, style to style — demonstrating fading recollection. Yet the final part of the poem opens:

> *I knew this; and I knew all summer long . . .*

Yet again, such certainty is deceptive. For though the first-person narrator works through the simple past, he and his aunt together are presented through the 'would' form that always, to some extent, replaces confident assertion with desire. The subversion of stanza and line continues, particularly in the last lines, where the power of the sentence asserts itself to suggest an impulse against form and towards fragmentation that, once again but more intensely, dramatizes the fate of memory:

> *One by one we would gather up the used jugs,*
> *   The glasses. We would pour away*
> *A little water. It would lie on the thick dust, gleaming.*

These lines make clear that, in these final three stanzas, the continued destabilizing devices are now supported by an important change of language. Events are now heightened, made luminous, idealized as the children encounter *the enormous experience of the mountain*. In particular:

> *In the summer, dust filled our winter ruts*
> *With a level softness, and children walked*
> *At evening through golden curtains scuffed*
> > *From the road by their trailing feet.*

They

> *. . . murmur slowly through our stiff*
> *Gate, their shy heads gilded by the last sun.*

Here, at the poem's heart, the once-marching children now drift away through curtains that, though beautiful, obscure vision, suggest finales, evoke night; made inanimate by *gilding*, they feel the *last sun*.

For the language of these final stanzas effects an imaginative transformation of the original memory. That memory, always unstable, uncertain, given shape only with difficulty, is now almost wholly lost in the glowing words of this closing part. And it is one of the modern strengths of the poem that Norris does not discuss or search explicitly for meaning. Rather, the poem in itself exhibits its insights into the nature of recollection. The final lines point to the pessimistic appropriateness of the title: *water*, unstable, ephemeral, sustaining, is an apt symbol for recollection. It represents what is left after the experience, gleaming momentarily before drying into the *thick dust* that is our common fate.

'Water', in its subtle, characteristic, and much

misunderstood way, is about the irrecoverable loss
of a world that is not wholly idyllic: the momentary
menace of *visionary gangs* is a potent suggestion.
For, in Norris's poetry, childhood is never without
its darker side. 'Dead Boys' is about a childhood
tragedy; in 'Skulls', slippery snow is remembered
and *Our pink bones. . ./Broken on that playground*. 'The
Ballad of Billy Rose' describes thoughtless
callousness as boys watch a beaten boxer lose his
sight — *but we were tough/And clapped him as they
wrapped his blindness up* — or, in 'The Strong Man',
applaud the tricks of a street-entertainer: *We/Cheered
his freedom: if such are free*. 'A Blunt Invasion', in which

> . . . *After the conventional words*
> *I slung my tight knuckles*
> *Hard as a stone*
> *Over his slow*
> *Left shoulder,*

explores the aggressively cruel rituals, the
physical and social tensions of an upbringing
that, for Norris and those like him, was always *a
blunt invasion of the better streets*. Further, this
often disturbing childhood world is one into
which the excluded adult can only peer. Thus, in
'Man and Boy', though the teacher offers
comfort, the grieving youngster remains *aloof and
alone in his oval of grief*, and the adult reflects
sadly, *I shall not cure his wounds, though my own
scars are burning*.

Norris's concern with childhood is part of a wider
obsession with the past. In 'A February Morning'
that past, *time out of mind ago, in Wales*, is a deep,
emotional experience the intensity and quality of

which enable it to be remembered in a calmer present. The past is a lost world with whose dead inhabitants he can feel affinity, as when, in 'A Sense of History', the sight of a damaged *crude mosaic* around a mountain lake compels him to identify with ancient workers:

> *I only know that I was suddenly kneeling . . .*
> *And plugging with scales of stone the wave-worn gaps.*

'The Twelve Stones of Pentre Ifan' celebrates the faith and labours of *the old ones* who built the cromlech. 'At the Sea's Edge, in Pembrokeshire', about the building of St David's Cathedral, is a further encounter with the long-dead, in this case with those ordinary men whose work became *a stone praise* and, in particular, Peter de Leia, the twelfth-century bishop who *saw stone/vault and flower*. Such concern with a strange, dead, working world full of intense feeling and firm Christian conviction stems from Norris's typically dualistic sense of himself as both inheritor and loser. He ends 'Old Voices':

> *. . . my hand*
> *In its perfect glove of skin holds*
> *Other ghosts. We step the streets*
> *Uneasily, disturbed by bells.*

But the past, like the childhood which it contains, is more often a terrible place, where Drummer Evans, *Hands flying high in volleys of retaliation*, sounded an old man's futile defiance against the poorhouse, where his godchild, James Chuang, was killed by a blocked air-vent, and where Lyn

James, that *cuffed and bleeding* boxer, died in the
ring. In 'An Old House', Norris remembers the
murder of a *struck girl in her ropes of blood.* 'Elegy
for David Beynon', the desperately moving poem
about Aberfan that celebrates the life and final
bravery of a teacher friend who died *in the
crushed school* in that *great anonymous tragedy,* in
part presents the past as a place of carnage.

Certainly it is full of dead writers. Alun Lewis is
celebrated lugubriously in the early 'Retreat for
Alun Lewis', Dylan Thomas in 'At the Grave of
Dylan Thomas', a slack poem over-influenced by
Yeats and included in THE LOUD WINTER. Edward
Thomas, a persisting influence since that first
teenage encounter in W.H. Smith's, is the subject of
two poems. In 'Ransoms' Norris's admiration of
the scale of Thomas's pessimistic insight undercuts
the disclaimer:

> . . . *I have my small despair*
> *And would not want your sadness; your truth,*
> *Your tragic honesty, are what I know you for.*

'A Glass Window, in Memory of Edward Thomas,
at Eastbury Church', is equally powerful and
revealing:

> *The path cut in the pane most worries me,*
> *. . . I turn away, knowing it is, for me,*
>
> *That sullen lane leading you out of sight,*
> *In darkening France.*

The second line troubles through its momentary
application to Norris himself. In 'A True Death',

Vernon Watkins, who lived where *a burnish/Of sea glinted at the world's edge*, is at the border of the known to which Norris is instinctively attracted. In 'His Last Autumn', an elegy for Andrew Young, Norris's neighbour and friend, death becomes, strangely and movingly, an escape from the cold. The famous literary dead — Auden, Watkins, Roethke and, particularly, Dylan Thomas — are remembered in 'A Reading in Seattle'. Afterwards:

> *The party over,*
> *I walked home, saw on peaks*
> *The coldest snow, white as bone.*

This final image, typically, is both beautiful and chilling. Most disturbing of all is the link between death and beauty established, in 'Looking at Snowdrops', when the poet and his wife

> *. . . step off the thin path*
> *Among lakes of the flowers.*
> *. . . So might*
> *That sauntering, sad Hart Crane, his*
> *Solid boat set far homeward in the seapaths,*
> *Have walked off into the waves.*

World War Two is central to remembrance. In 'An Old House' he writes of the frightened boys:

> *Five simple years soon took them to the war*
> *That burned their vision on all Europe's houses.*
> *In the old house it was their death they saw.*

His friend, *Golden David*, recalled in 'Picking

Coal', was *soon to die in exploding Europe.*
'Autumn Elegy' is a commemoration:

> *Young men of my own time died*
> *In the Spring of their living and could not turn*
> *To this. They died in their flames, hard*
> *War destroyed them.*

In 'Islands' he remembers

> *. . . Reg Smith, only child*
> *of old parents, his body*
> *wrapped in khaki, burned away*
> *and vanished in his smoke.*

There is no doubting Norris's compassion. But the war references make clear what is implicit in so many of his other engagements with the past: he is fascinated by and attracted towards death and destructive violence. Thus, for example, *They died in their flames, hard/War destroyed them* invests those deaths, that violence, with mythic glamour. Those who regard Norris as little more than a latter-day Georgian should keep such moments in mind.

They should also think carefully about his concern with nature. His nature poetry, influenced by his admiration for Andrew Young, has always been distinguished by detailed, accurate observation, as, for example, in 'A February Morning':

> *. . . the frost-hung fields where the mild cattle*
> *Stand wreathed in their own breath, I watch smooth*
> *Starlings, loud handfuls of shot silk*

or the superb *butterflies prancing* in 'Man and Boy', or, from 'Berries':

> *round crab, the seeds of spindle*
>
> *and wayfarer, clusters of buttery haw,*
> *the waxy barberry, the black lamps*
>
> *of ivy, beads of neglected briar,*
> *of alder buckthorn, succulent*
>
> *candle of yew.*

Elsewhere is a deeper interest in nature as a harsher, more fundamental world. As he writes in 'The Old Year':

> *. . . I am reluctant*
> *To leave the warm house . . .*
> *. . . Yet I should stand*
> *Under a deep tree in a field of frost fire,*
> *Hearing the call of owls.*

Once again he stands in one world — civilized, warm, *Behind many hedges and in tufted country* — and stares, rapt and, at times, appalled, into an alien existence. In 'Curlew', when he hears the *delicate non-humanity* of its cry he knows that

> *. . . this adamant bird*
> *With the plaintive throat and curved, uneasy jaws*
> *Crying creates a desert with a word*
>
> *More terrible than chaos, and we stand at the edge*
> *Of nothing.*

Norris responds to nature's hostile power: *Winter branched in me, ice cracked/In my bleeding*, he writes

in 'Early Frost'; in 'Midwinter', he records the
violence of a storm:

> . . . *Great blows of snow*
> *Swing on a blind wind as the staggering*
> *Morning lurches itself half alive.*

In 'Now the House Sleeps' that hostility is again
made explicit: *the ring of hills wears light/Of
morning like a steel helmet.* Finding the source of
that hostility returns us to violence. Thus, in
'Buzzard' Norris enters Ted Hughes country:

> *He is not without pity for he does not know pity.*
> *He is a machine for killing; searchlight eye,*
> *Immaculate wing, then talon and hook.*
> *He kills without cruelty for he does not know cruelty.*

Paradoxically, the matter-of-fact tone intensifies
our sense of the extent to which Norris is drawn
towards amoral destructiveness.

He moves readily and often into brutal language.
Thus, in 'Space Miner', *encrusted ore . . . had ripped/
Strips from his flesh*; elsewhere, as in 'Shadows', the
faces of fishermen gaffing a salmon . . . *stared red,/
Reflecting/His gashed blood*, polecats commit *tearing
murder* and, in 'Clymping, Sussex', he sees the
setting sun *Lie in a long blood*. 'October Sun',
powerful, disturbing, is even more revealing:

> *Sun, wild October sun, unleash your lions.*
> *Send them from brazen Africa, let them lean*
> *Into my garden . . .*
> *. . . Let them invade my eyes,*
> *I shall cage them behind my lashes.*

Blake's tiger has become Norris's lions: natural violence is welcomed and, as the *lashes* image suggests, stimulates his own. In 'Grooming', the poem itself becomes the lion and the poetic task one of vicious devastation:

> ... *I'll set it*
> *wild on the running street, aimed*
> *at the hamstring, the soft throat.*

In Norris's poetry lost childhood, the past, nature, the creative life, are darkened, dangerous, beckoning worlds, feelings summed up in two Blakean lines from 'Now the House Sleeps':

> *But at the edge of what I know*
> *The massed, appalling forests grow.*

His vantage-point in the shifting present undergoes changes in locale: 'Merthyr' poems give way to 'Sussex' poems, British settings to American. It remains a place of love occasionally explored, as in 'Cardigan Bay', 'Moonman' and, particularly, as defying physical decline, in 'Unchanging':

> ... *The world's*
> *Grown calcinous. What miracle, when*
> *That which we call the heart is still*
> *Immutable constancy, unchanged love.*

It can also be a place of faith, evident in 'Christmas Day' and in the beautiful late poem, 'Christmas in Utah', where

Higher than snowpeaks,
shriller than the frost,
a brazen angel blows his silent trumpet.

Norris celebrates practised skills, such as driving, fishing and swimming; he savours the delights of warm bathing and the beauties of nature, both brought together in 'Travelling West':

> *. . . I hung*
> *In a hammock of water, warm silt soft*
> *To the toes. Mallard*
> *Feathered above my comfort, the long*
> *Westering light streamed through the red oaks.*

He gains great pleasure from birds and animals, from dogs, horses, and 'The Beautiful Young Devon Shorthorn Bull, Sexton Hyades 33rd', through whom *The far fields fill with his children, his soft daughters.* All help celebrate a life become comfortable in material terms. It is a life of fine clothes, of which, in 'An Evening by the Lake', he is self-mockingly aware:

> *. . . A check*
> *Overcoat, fresh from the cleaners,*
> *Discreet suede shoes, (I use a wire brush),*
> *Trouser-legs, that new bronze-green colour,*
> *Just narrow enough for good taste.*

'Postcards from Wales' describes his Cardiganshire retreat, to which he will return

> *On some afternoon warm and loving, to a handful*

Of fields by Teifi river and a cottage blind
       With waiting.

He is sometimes sustained by memory, as when
the smell of ransoms brings thoughts of Edward
Thomas and a sense of poetic kinship, so that, *as
I / . . . Drive slowly down the hill, I'm comforted.* This
happy present so often seems escapist, limbo-
like, an alternative to a troubled past or
intimations of a disturbed future. 'Bridges'
makes the point:

> *. . . I rarely cross right over,*
> *Preferring to stand, watching the grain*
> *On running water. I like such bridges best,*
> *River bridges on which men always stand,*
> *In quiet places.*

If this was Norris's only stance — cosily looking
away, looking down — he would not be much
regarded. His present is more complex, not only
because of the dark shadows of childhood, the
past, and the natural world, but because of two
other hauntings. First, he cannot escape a sense
of loss and apprehension that is not only
personal — *savaged/By creatures of my own failure*
— and fearful —

> *What if the great lines never come; I have*
> *The cold despair of searching for them*

— and a consequence of being a *discovered alien*,
but also social, as when, in 'Rome Remembered',
he confronts the ruined Merthyr of his upbring-
ing where

> Rome stands in the raw towers
> Of fallen steelworks, her eagle
> Sails on the walls of sacked blast-furnaces,
> Cinders cover her emperors.

Secondly, because his fine work has come late in life to stay very late, it is oppressed by an ominous future:

> I sit alert in the still room, hearing
> The storm, knowing no end to the journey,

or, after 'Driving Home',

> When I have done I will sit in the orderly dark,
> Waiting for what will come to me, what is to come.

Ill, lying awake, he feels:

> Almost the final terror, my lungs boiling,
> Tongue too big for talk, mouth
> Tasting the body's bitter dissolution;
> Aware of death.

Norris's present is a world *heavy with dying* in which he is increasingly conscious of his own ageing. 'Lear at Fifty' (included in WATER MUSIC, published in Norris's fiftieth year), the title fiercely suggestive of the helpless foolishness of declining years, explores this state of mind.

The poem begins, on a frosty autumn morning, by asserting the power of the machine over the natural: the unthinking narrator, in his *Glib metal*, not only *driving [through] the lanes* but *driving the lanes [before him]*. With him comes the destructive sun, *burning*

. . . away the *frost fur* that reverses conventional responses by making cold seem comforting. Such powerful and destructive elements drive into the poem through a long, periodic sentence accumulating force against an *old man, sweeping leaves together*, weakly predicated by the main verb. There are no precise rhymes, only hints, using *i* and *s*, at assonantic links; the sentence overwhelms the lines and the shape of the stanza. With stanza one itself struggling to exist as a coherent shape, the opening lines enact rather than describe the vulnerability of age.

From the end of stanza one to line two of stanza three the stanzas remain subservient to sentences that shorten and in which angular diction, as, for example, *He shifted his/Feet to careful standing*, counters progression. The old man is befuddled with sleep; his movements are ponderous; his broom is *his necessary crutch* that

> *. . . moved like an*
> *Insect on slow, frail, crawling legs from*
> *Leaf to leaf.*

He is dehumanized, stripped of dignity, at the mercy of circumstances: the car passing ruins his labour, *heaps of the dry/Work spilling and flying*.

The old man's arid, enervated world is replaced, suddenly, by the tremendous energy of rough, heavily polluted seas:

> *Waves, unexpected heavy waves*
> *From some wild, piling storm away at sea,*
> *Ripped the mild sand, smashed rocks, and shot the*
> *Squalling gulls out of the filth, vomit*

And glittering sewage . . .   55
  Old shoes, cans, cynical gouts of accidental oil,
    Plastic bottles, ropes, bubbling detergent
  Slime, all were thrown to the sea wall.

Such lines restate violently the quieter opening
contrast between vulnerability and hostile
circumstances. The old man is a victim. He is
part of the detritus of a society that forces all
such to 'the [sea] wall'; his futile attempts at
ordering mirror the community's. Norris links
the polluted sea and the man's predicament:

                    I have
      No wish to remember those unwelcoming

    Waves I turned my back on, nor to think of old men
      Sitting tight in their skulls, aghast
    At what their soft, insistent mouths will keep on
      Yelling.

Here is a third connection: between the old men
yelling and the squalling gulls. Both depend
upon society's leavings; both, the old men and
the *flung birds*, are controlled by greater forces,
natural as well as man-made. But the sea is also
death, smashing against the *limpet hours* of
clinging mortality; Norris, walking *the fields as if
on a cliff's edge,/The idea of flight in me*, senses his
own gull-like fate and contemplates suicide.
Aged fifty, he is a younger Lear who can
visualize the despairing, foolish senility of later
life: *my/Friends, myself . . . turned/Sticks, turned
tottering old fools.* Sunset brings a sickly *yellow
light* and *A false warmth.* The conclusion is
despairing:

In the morning some old man will start
To sweep his leaves to a neatness.

The old are the lowly, the impersonalized (*some old man*), who only *start* tasks. The swept leaves — suggesting, additionally, the writer struggling with his pages and so associating Norris with the bleak conclusion — will inevitably be scattered by the *Glib metal* of a hostile world.

As memory fades and nature's beauties seem overwhelmed by destructive energies, Norris visualizes an even more disturbing alternative. This world to come is defamiliarized not only by reversing usual responses and by the barely contained fragmenting impulse effected by the shaping sentences, but also by means of deviating syntax. Hence the immediate strangeness of, for example, *This morning early* and *the flung birds flocked for*. Added to this are abrupt changes of subject, such as the shift from the leaves *spilling and flying* to *Nobody walked on the shore*, violent diction and the subtle ambiguity of Norris's writing. Like his vision of the past in, say, 'Water', that of the future is equally disconcerting, a strange, uncertain world, and a shockingly sudden view of terrible senility.

The fragmenting impulse, the abruptness, lead him, perhaps naturally, to the poem-sequence that began with 'Poem in Ten Parts' and 'Speaking to Friends'. 'Nightingales' and 'Two Men' are sequential gestures; ISLANDS OFF MAINE (1977) shows Norris seizing firmly the form that dominates his later career. It was reprinted, slightly revised, in WATER VOICES, which also includes 'Cave Paintings', a second American sequence.

In eight short lyrics of unrhymed and irregular
couplets or triplets unified by a tone of wary
excitement, 'Cave Paintings' explores a central
Norris theme, the relationship between the civilized
and the primitive. The sound of police sirens,
pebbles that recall *voices of moist caves*, a thrush
trapped in a room, memories of an ancestor who
first left the *brutal soil*, are among moments that
recall the atavistic memory, symbolized by the
cave, which fades all too quickly:

> *. . . For*
> *The cave is filling, fills*
>
> *Rapidly. It closes,*
> *From the eyes in.*

'Islands Off Maine' is more complex, though, like
'Cave Paintings', it begins with noises out of
darkness: before dawn a man is heard hammer-
ing *From his home on crevices/Shatters the darkness.*
In the early light

> *Water smooth as claws*
> *Holds its silent traps;*
> *On the visible tide*
> *Floats huge America.*

Mysterious, urgent, dark-destroying sound, a
precarious house, deceptive hostile nature, a
looming continent: this opening section points to
the sequence's central concern with an island and
its community under threat. The second poem
stresses the menacing indifference of nature:
cruel ospreys, who *carry their fish head first, a
torpedo*, ignore the complaints of other birds and

regard the island as no more than a part of their geographical pattern of existence. In the third, the *mad boy* is, as it were, the spirit of the island, a latter-day Caliban :

> *Brambles had torn his jeans,*
> *His fingers were harsh as carrots,*
> *Waterbeads dropped in his bull's curls.*

Screaming like a blue jay, he is aggressive towards visitors to this alien world:

> *Why don't you leave? If you knew*
> *The people here, you'd leave today!*

Even *Unseen gulls jeered . . . when I hit the dirt path.*

Poems four and five explore the island's history. Pink Harding is the oldest inhabitant, turning always to the past, custodian of a tradition become museum-bound. The poem that follows is about the dead, in particular about Gilman U. Stanley, aged sixteen, who, in 1861, drowned off Newfoundland during his first whaling voyage:

> *. . . The sea took him, pressed flat*
>
> *His agile breath, swam him among rocks*
> *In water blue as ice . . .*

Now, nature moves *like a slow green tide on his empty grave,/ . . . and the other headstones.*

In five short lyrics Norris re-creates an old, isolated, island community of craftsmen and sailors, now in decline. He ends with bell-buoys, reminders of nautical danger:

> *water tongue*
> *clapper and safe hammer*
> *sea's elegy and sound*
>
> *celebrate our passing*
>
> *toll for us.*

In Norris's hands the sequence is ideal for the representation of decline. For though there are some unifying elements, such as the abiding presence of the sea and the general movement towards ageing and death, the part dominates, this in itself suggesting breakup. This last is further dramatized by the replacement of regular form — the first five poems are in unrhymed quatrains or triplets — by the exploded, fragmented structure of the final poem. Things fall apart, which is what the elegy mourns through enactment.

Norris's late collection, A SEA IN THE DESERT (1989), consists almost wholly of three sequences. Indeed, the American edition, lacking two separate poems, 'A Sea in the Desert' and 'Decoys', is called, simply, SEQUENCES (1988).

'The Dark Months' brings together five poems from various points in Norris's career. Two, 'Christmas in Utah' and 'The Dark Months', are superb examples of the spare, taut, compressed style characteristic of his best work during the 1980s. The diffuse nostalgia of the other three are reminders of how much his work has changed. The five are too uneven in quality and too stylistically disparate to prevent the group from being less than the sum of its parts.

'Stones Trees Water' consists of forty-one variations on the otherness of nature, that perennial Norris theme. The longest is eighteen short lines, the shortest is three. Each is a fragment, a momentary impression, compressed, unrhymed and self-contained. The overall tone is generally sombre but varied by moments of lyrical beauty, deeper sadness and occasional questioning that increase the sense of fragmentation. Within each part the line is the dominant unit, often breaking up sentences into short, separated phrases, as in part 13, about trees in winter:

> *They are turned now*
> *from the wind*
> *that shaped their growing*
> *and it is enough*
> *that they endure*
> *what each day's weather*
> *brings to them.*

Nature is often a source of delight:

> *To live with water. To walk over*
> *water meadows, to know the seasons*
> *of change and renewal in the colonies.*

Invariably it is a source of aesthetic pleasure, as in the beech wood of part 8:

> *. . . when light*
> *is perfect green, underwater colour,*

> *green of sunlight filtered*
> *through prodigal green leaves, our hands*
> *and upturned paler faces green*

or when

> *Green winter sun touches the yearning poplars.*
> *. . . And high in the sudden luminous*
> *blue of the revealed sky, see there, the pale*
> *enigmatic symbol of the daylight moon.*

But the main stress is on nature's mysterious and often aggressive power. At times this is latent: *an elm and three quiet elms far off,/poised for dancing.* Invariably it is real but imagined, as with the known response to spring, the roots' slow, unseen growth from *the first pale/tendrils,* its *great fist/clamped about rock and cavity,* and in the *sharp, clear statement* of a cliff, or the sea's *gouged/sockets* in its rocks. Often it is sexual, as with the sea's *wet buss/on the curves/of firm stone,* or when

> *Water*
> *wears at the long orifices*
> *of stone, grinds honeycombs*
> *of entrances into the hard body*
> *of rock.*

Nature is celebrated. The relationship between nature and man is more variable. A dry-stone wall has to be built skilfully, *the earth/has to accept it* or else it *breaks its dry bonds, topples it.* More importantly, Norris's concern with man's treatment of the environment, first prominent in 'Lear at Fifty', now re-emerges powerfully:

Fire, the acid exhalation
of industrial chimneys, serpentine
breeding of highways: the trees
are dead.

And,

. . . Our scum
floats at the edge of water, clings
to the stones on the shore.

Although,

. . . in casual pattern we search
for meaning, for significant omens.
But a wind ruffles the water's face,

yet in the seasonal movement our own sad
progress is prefigured, so that, eventually:

Revealed by winter, small trees
stand like rueful old men,
their bare shanks thin, their
old veins hardening.

In deep midwinter our sense of disaster goes far
beyond the personal:

We walk the broken wood
as through another war. Winter
rehearses the end of the world.

Here is no comforting anthropomorphism;
Norris is far away from Wordsworthian

sustenance. The fragmenting effect of the
sequence, neutralizing such unifying devices as
the use of the sea or the general tone, prevents
any accumulating sense of existential harmony.
Though prefiguring counters the 'otherness' of
nature to an extent not previously seen in
Norris's poetry yet his evocation of nature's
tremendous power keeps that natural world as
an impossible alternative. For the sequence ends,
first with a poet's death — Shelley's cremation *on
the Pisan shore* — linked to Norris's through his
own, ironical, *celebratory fire*, and, secondly, with
a final image of helplessness:

> *I stand at the land's edge, waiting*
> *for what the tide will bring to me*
> *and what it will take away.*

'The Hawk's Eye', which opens A SEA IN THE
DESERT, is his finest sequence. Its eight lyrics
contrast the hawk's world with the human.
Though Norris has written elsewhere — in 'Buz-
zard' and 'Islands off Maine' — of nature red in
tooth and claw, this is not now his purpose. For
though we are reminded of the hawk's cruel
potential (*the cross of my shadow/closes a wood of
singers*), in 'The Hawk's Eye' the bird inhabits a
very different world. The hawk *knows the quiet
architecture/of high places*. It waits *in blue light, for/
early thermals*. It

> *. . . ignores*
> *the political world,*
> *is concerned with what's visible.*

His own world is valued as a superb observatory where

> *Counties are opening under me,*
>
> *in daylight, for my regard*

and where

> *My eye measures*
> *the edges of the world.*

The hawk not only sees natural creatures and features but also humans, where and how they live. He sees a world different from and worse than his own airy spaces. If I was a hawk, writes the narrator, looking down on *dark farms/in the huddle of winter,*

> *I could see the men*
> *I might have become*
> *turn out of their stiff clothes*
> *to sleep the cold night, fatigued.*

For the human world is presented as a dreadful place of dispossession, rootlessness, cruelty, where the compassionate young will *run screaming/from the slaughterhouse* and suffer *brutal labour in furnaces*. It is a world of devitalizing pollution and indifference to natural beauty:

> *One tractor hangs the pale*
>
> *of its exhaust against a hedge.*
> *. . . And in the meadows*
> *cruel children hunt among flowers.*

When the hawk ventures unwarily into this
world it is destroyed:

> *The one purpose*
> *of her gaze*
> *will not let her see*
> *the clear windscreen*
> *moving to kill her . . .*
>
> *She dies at the roadside.*

The hawk's world, then, is juxtaposed to our own. We are returned to Norris's characteristic stance. And though his scathing attitude to how we live has been a dominant theme from 'Lear at Fifty' onwards, in 'The Hawk's Eye' three factors make this more than restatement. First, the viewpoint shifts between that of the narrator and that of the narrator-as-hawk, making possible the development of an important sub-theme. *I look through the hawk's lens/for an essence I guess at,* writes the narrator. That *essence,* in 'Hawk Music', is

> *. . . a sound*
>
> *so high the ear cannot*
> *support it. But I*
> *will hope to hear it.*

The hawk, that is, stands for the poet in action. Norris's early concern with the latter's role is explored once more but with greater clarity and assurance. Here, he writes — seeking to reconcile detail with panorama, searching, idealistically, obsessively, for *that green/country which put an end to time* — that *I begin to organise my patterns.* The poet cherishes the hope that, after death,

I shall leave a cry
hanging beyond echo
in the sustenance of air.

Secondly, though in his early work and from
time to time in the poetry of his maturity Norris
has evoked religious awareness, this is not now
the case. The aggressive solipsism of the hawk,
the solipsistic desires of the poet, are subject only
to stronger natural forces. *It is the snow brings him
down*, we are soon told of the bird who can
otherwise rise *higher than winter*. And, in the end,
the seasons/took him, for all his mastery. In this late
work Norris, once again, writes with a disturbing
secularity.

This registers more deeply and darkly because,
thirdly, in this tightly unified sequence — even
'Hudson's Geese' can be read as a gloss on the *wild
geese* section of the preceding 'The Hawk Maps His
Country', a close encounter with some aspects of
that harsh world above which the hawk rises — the
quality of the writing is uniformly high, a fine
example of Norris's late style. A brief example from
'The Summer Hawk' must serve to illustrate the
point:

> *I wait in blue light, for*
> *early thermals, a hint*
> *of lift. My arms stretch*
>
> *in effortless recognition, in*
> *widening order at the day's turn.*

The involuntary, momentary pauses induced
after *for* and *hint* mirror hovering; *effortless*

recognition re-enacts stretching; *order* not only suggests arrangement but also appropriate power. In *the day's turn* are suggestions of the hawk's circling movement, the slow revolving of the earth and subservient waiting. All the while the speaking voice persists, as does the controlled power of the compressed lines. In these late sequences, setting aside differences in subject-matter, Norris has some affinities with the intensely spare utterance of R.S. Thomas's later work: the pressure of felt and often pessimistic emotion has stripped away all but essentials, leaving hard, gem-like language still embodying, miraculously, the sound of the speaking voice that gives it, so often, a piercing emotional charge.

IV

When Leslie Norris's fiction first flowered he was well established as a poet. Given the strong relationship between the lyric poem and the short story, it was perhaps inevitable that he should turn, exclusively, to that fictional form. And, since the poem-sequence has always been important to him, it comes as no surprise to discover that, though he does not write stories with an eye on relationship, when collecting them for publication he has been concerned with order and arrangement. He has written of SLIDING:

I tried to arrange the stories so that they resonated against each other, so that they were more than a sum of their parts.

It follows then that, certainly in SLIDING, each Norris story is only 'complete' in its final context. Because of this and because he sometimes revises published stories before collecting them — 'Sing it Again, Wordsworth' is an example — discussion of Norris's fiction is restricted to the two collections, SLIDING (1978) and THE GIRL FROM CARDIGAN (1988), which include about half of his fictional output.

SLIDING begins with two stories about childhood in a Welsh valley. Both involve initiations, sudden encounters with new experiences. In the opening story, 'Waxwings', seven-year-old Alwyn for the first time in his life wanders on to the hills above his home. After various small adventures with a young

man and a dog he continues upwards, beyond
people. As he walks through a hawthorn wood the
waxwings arrive, *glittering birds* in search of food:

*Ripping in hundreds through the dry twigs of the
hawthorns, they tore and devoured the scarlet berries with
ferocious, brittle energy ... Their heads held crests of
chestnut, a black stripe ran dramatically through each eye,
their bodies were tinged with pink ...*

Here is the story's climax, an experience that
includes aesthetic delight in closely observed
natural detail, fascination with violence, and in-
tense imaginative response and transformation:

*[The birds] were so brilliant that the boy cried his delight
aloud, holding out his arms to them ... He thought they
were like hundreds of candles sparkling through the trees.*

Alwyn returns home to a worried, angry, though
ultimately relieved and understanding mother,
to a world of mundane circumstances that
contrasts with his mind's *marvellous vision of the
waxwings*, a vision that he cannot find words to
express.

'Waxwings' is followed by the title story, 'Sliding',
about eight-year-old Bernard. The basic structure
is the same: a movement upwards from home in the
valley on to the mountain, a movement away from
the warmth and secure comfort of home into a
world of excitement and adventure. In midwinter
Bernard and his friends go sliding on a frozen pond
above the town. At first they are daunted by
bleakness: *Featureless, the ice stretched on, swept by
an unhindered wind. The boys bent their heads down
against the brutal cold.* But delight in satisfying
physical activity and in ordered companionship in

a group with a dominant leader, counters the weather, so that *Bernard thought he had never seen anything as lovely as the dark ice . . . and the still figures of his friends.* But Danny falls and loses consciousness. Frightened boys build a fire to warm him, cheer when he revives. Chastened, they return home. As they reach the town they start to run:

They trotted close together, moving home as one boy through the darkness, united against whatever terror might threaten them.

The third story, 'Cocksfoot, Crested Dog's Tail, Sweet Vernal Grass', is similar in that it is about the potency of childhood memory and confronting new experiences. In other respects it is very different. Instead of concentrating on one significant moment, the story summarizes a man's life from age thirteen, when his father died, through various mainly dishonest vicissitudes until, in his fifties, he is a rich property speculator. The story, set on the south coast of England, is sad and amoral, charting abrupt changes of direction and the ready relinquishing of personal relationships. But the unemotional factuality with which the narrator tells his tale is ultimately belied by his memories. His life is haunted by his father's death and the funeral at which he first became aware of the grasses that give the story its title. His father's death dominates his middle age, the recollection of his childhood world, those *old, intangible summers,* growing more intense and lovely as his need for remembered roots presses more insistently:

I'll never go back; I know that.

Lately though, at night, on the edge of sleep, when the mind is undefended, I have seen again those grasses at the cemetery's verge more vividly fresh and green than they were long ago ... They hold themselves quietly for my recognition, and I make a ceremony of their names.

'The Highland Boy' returns us to Welsh valley life. Its lightly humorous tone contrasts with that of the first three stories. The hero is the young narrator's greyhound, whose unpredictable running usually reduces races to chaos. Unexpectedly, in an important race and to its backers' expensive chagrin, it beats the local favourite owned by the narrator's uncle. The lightness does not obscure two important concerns. First, the story juxtaposes the human world that tries to act with sense and logic to the instinctive, impulsive, unfathomable world of the animal, over which it can exercise little control. Secondly, the human world has its own instinctive impulse, appearing when sense and logic founder: Uncle Cedric fights all who question his integrity, which means, at the end of this story, those who will not accept Highland Boy's erratic nature.

When Uncle Cedric informs doubting Carl Jenkins that he will *push your nose through the back of your neck and tie your lying mouth in a knot*, the point is made humorously. But the concern with violence dominates more darkly the next two stories. The adult narrator of 'The Mallard', a story set in rural southern England, was a keen boxer when a boy but gave up the sport when he discovered he could not control himself. Now, a recalcitrant neighbour shoots a wild duck from the narrator's pond:

I'd hit him twice before his fist had finished his backswing, and a slow trickle of blood came from his nose. Then suddenly I was crouching and weaving, my left hooking him to head and body so hard I thought he'd snap. Whatever it was I had thought buried in me was not dead.

The story ends despairingly with the man not knowing what to do. 'A Big Night', with its Valley setting, is on the same theme. A keen schoolboy boxer attends a professional championship fight. A friend breaks an arm trying to climb in without paying; the boy watches the fight's cold ferocity. Both moments of violence affect him deeply. When next in the gym, sparring with his friend Charlie Nolan, he loses control:

Charlie was bleeding from the mouth and nose and he was pawing away with his gloves open. I could tell he was frightened. Yet I kept on ripping punches at him, my hands suddenly hard and urgent . . .

The fight is stopped; the boy never boxes again.

This sudden, shocking change of mood darkens the reader's sense of the stories that follow. 'A House Divided', set in the Carmarthenshire of Norris's ancestors, evokes a pre-war Eden of wonderful fishing and happy community life shattered by the war and by cynical deception, so that the narrator, leaving for ever in the rain, sees the *wide and jocund* Towy shining *like an enormous snail track*.

'Three Shots for Charlie Betson', arguably the volume's great achievement, is about a despairing need for roots. In a small Sussex village the Betsons are governed by instinct and natural forces; like animals or birds, they need familiar territory and a controlling hierarchy. When Charlie Betson marries he moves ten miles away to live in his wife's village but keeps returning obsessively. Early one morning, back in his birthplace, he shoots himself. His mother explains:

'He was a good boy,' she said, 'but he was lost. He needed safety . . . like their father before them . . . My boys need to be in the fields about us . . .'

Apart from rootlessness the story explores other disturbing areas of human psychology. Again, violence is one; whether accidental, as when the schoolteacher is killed in a car-crash, or a dog run down by a truck, or instinctive, such as Bill Francis's love of fighting and Charlie's resort to the shot-gun, it is a persistent social presence. A sub-theme is childlessness, suggesting the narrator's own and exploring that of Bill Francis, who, like the narrator, channels unspent paternalism into kindness to neighbours, public service and links with the local school. In Bill Francis's hatred of the Betsons we see the bitter side of his physiological predicament. As Charlie puts it, *'My father had nine boys . . . Bill Francis never had any. There ain't no Francis left.'* For the Betsons represent an ancient, continuing, fecund, vital, natural tradition at the heart of country life, inimical to modern patterns of living.

In 'Snowdrops' we return to childhood in Wales. This beautiful, lyrical story is about a small boy longing to see snowdrops in the school garden and, when he does, understanding their fragility and fortitude in the face of harsh circumstances:

He saw them blow in a sudden gust of the cold March wind, shake, and straighten gallantly . . . holding bravely to their specks of whiteness.

They offer a consoling possibility for the bereaved young schoolteacher grieving for her dead lover as his funeral passes the school-yard. But the boy, like the other frightened children, can hardly understand, for the story also dramatizes the difference between the separate worlds of the child and the adult. The former is a series of adventures and imaginative transformations, the latter a sad reality so often harrowed by death.

'Snowdrops' is followed by 'Prey', set in Sussex and in essence a series of anecdotes about hawks connected by the narrative persona. The narrator responds to a world in which the hawk can *fulfil his simple, orderly purpose* and, significantly for the sequence, is attracted by its violence. When trying to save small birds the narrator inadvertently drives them into a hawk's path: *I should have pitied those torn birds, but I was elated, elated.*

'A Moonlight Gallop' is also about Norris's boyhood; in making an excursion into the Gothic it further darkens the book's atmosphere. Three friends cycle to what is almost certainly Llanthony Abbey in Gwent. They stay at a nearby farm and are awoken during the night by the sound of a boy being exercised on a rope in the farmyard:

Round and round he went, his heavy boots thumping and sparking on the cobbles, in and out of the revealing light. His face as he raced towards us was empty, an idiot's face;

froth was forming around his mouth. Every time he raced
into the dark, he screamed his shaken cry.

Frightened, they leave next day. Thirty years later the narrator returns. As he walks through the ruined abbey he remembers *Charlie Bond who was killed in Africa in 1942 and Del Wellington who lives somewhere near Manchester and is a chemist.* The dominant memories are of adulthood with its tragedies and separations. He drives to the farm:

It was a warm day, full of summer, but momentarily all I saw were the lucid moonlight and the faces of my two friends, as clear as my hand; all I heard was a ragged galloping over the cobbles.

The response is ambiguous: *all* might mean the dominance of memory, but could mean 'unimportance', suggesting that, in the face of adult experience even that intense boyhood experience now seems less powerful.

'Away Away in China' is also concerned with the past's fading importance. An elderly bachelor, rich and successful, returns to his roots in west Wales, only to discover that time has moved on, his experiences have been superseded, he has even lost his cherished power to patronize. His past has become lost and strange, like the *so alien, so foreign* world of the birds he sees from the train. On his first night in his sister's house, old and irrelevant, *he lay still and straight in the bed as a scatter of unexpected rain hit the pane, irregular, hard, stinging like tears.* The penultimate story, 'A Roman Spring', is about protecting a west Wales property, exploring the past and sustaining memory. It ends with the narrator excavating an ancient spring, part of his growing understanding of the property's history.

'Percy Colclough and the Religious Girls', ends the book by effecting an abrupt change of mood. Its lighter tone recalls 'The Highland Lad' and, like the earlier story, depends on a jokey ending: religious Percy and his friend, both from Aberdare, visit Swansea to meet girls, Percy taking his Bible in case he spends the night with one and could not return in time for chapel at home. Comparatively, the story is a trivial one. It is presented as a slice of real life told to the narrator, in a Sussex pub, by the man who had accompanied Percy to Swansea. The ending completes the realistic frame in a manner similar, for example, to that of Dylan Thomas's 'Old Garbo'. When told of the story the friend laughs. *'It's all true,' he said, 'Every word of it'* and adds that when *'Percy Colclough found out that those two girls were also religious he was white with anger'*.

Except that the first two stories are about childhood SLIDING is not arranged in any kind of chronological sequence. Nor is it organized in terms of setting, moving in arbitrary fashion from south Wales to Sussex to west Wales. Structures are varied. The narrative stance shifts from omniscience in, for example, 'Waxwings', to the first-person or to third-person narration strictly from a single character's point of view. Rather, the stories are united by thematic concerns: the need for roots, the power of the past, the attractions of violence, the concerns, that is to say, of his finest poetry. SLIDING develops such ideas, as it does, of course, the basic concept, implicit in the title, of a precarious existence in an ordered, controlled world that is always close to disorder, the wild and perhaps disaster.

Certainly violence is a central theme; the extent to which it fascinates the young is established in the first two stories, in 'Waxwings', as has been noted, in 'Sliding' in part by describing Danny's fall in slow motion:

They saw his heels leave the ice, and for a perceptible moment he sailed through the unsupporting air before the back of his head cracked frighteningly against the surface. He lay broken and huddled.

'The Highland Boy', through Uncle Cedric, 'The Mallard' and 'A Big Night' treat violence as an integral part of the human character, the latter two stressing its often uncontrollable nature. 'Three Shots for Charlie Betson' shows violence and the physically instinctive life to be always close to, sometimes uneasily within, the civilized human world. 'Prey' helps sustain this notion of closeness and that of the attraction of violence through the final part of the volume.

Again, a sense of the intense potency of childhood memories, the subject-matter of the first two stories, is also developed through the sequence though, in this case, in unexpected fashion. The force of such memories, insisted upon in, for example, 'A Big Night' and 'A House Divided', and very directly in 'Cocksfoot, Crested Dog's-Tail, Sweet Vernal Grass', is partly subverted at the close of 'A Midnight Gallop' and wholly undermined in 'Away Away in China', as Alan Gwyther finds the past increasingly meaningless through a lonely retirement. Indeed, memory itself, as dramatized by the changing focus of these tales, from person to person, from one time and place to another — 'Three Shots for Charlie Betson', for example, in which the action immediately precedes the writing of it, is followed by 'Snowdrops', recalling a long-gone Merthyr childhood — becomes shifting, uncertain, blurred at times, an effect compounded within some stories — 'Waxwings' for instance — through a point of view that flickers from child to omniscient adult.

Essentially, these stories portray a series of familiar juxtapositions: alongside the ordinary, mundane world are strange, sinister, often threatening worlds of instinct, animality, amoral savagery and, importantly, imaginative promise. Alongside the adult world is that of children, who inhabit a glowing, intense, though not always reassuring plane of existence. This is not to say that Norris's short stories are more poems in prose, for two basic differences are apparent. Both are consequences of fictiveness. First, Norris's poetry is invariably direct, 'confessional' in approach. Though he occasionally adopts overt personae, as, for example, in 'The Old Age of Llywarch Hen' or 'Siencyn ap Nicolas upon his Death-Bed', almost always his is a personal poetry the narrator of which may well be Norris himself; the experience seems authentic, merging, it appears, with that of the reader. But the stories are recognizably *stories*, with narrative, characters, and various, clearly characterized narrators. These fictional worlds are always slightly distanced, demonstrated, and enacting, in their links with their readers, that main concern with strange worlds juxtaposed. Here the second difference is important and involves the final story, 'Percy Colclough and the Religious Girls'. Its lighter tone, its triviality, its dependence on a contrived concluding joke and, above all, the over-insistence on it being a true story that succeeds only in reminding us that it is fiction drains tension and emotional anguish from our reading. We are made to realize that we have only been reading stories. But 'only' is double-edged: we do not forget that we have been emotionally involved, disturbed, troubled by a darkening sequence. We know, that is to say, that we have participated in serious imaginative involvement in worlds different from our own. We end this superb sequence conscious of living in one world but glimpsing another that, though near and powerful, remains apart and always strange.

Taken as a whole THE GIRL FROM CARDIGAN is less impressive. The American edition contained sixteen stories; the British edition has twenty and it has to be said that the four additions do not strengthen the volume. Two are unconvincing excursions into the supernatural. 'All You Who Come to Portland Bill' is simply a creepy contrivance about a man seeing his own name on a gravestone. 'Johnny Trevecca and the Devil' is a more interesting failure. As a story about culture clash in the Merthyr of Norris's childhood — the young narrator becoming friends with a tough boy from a poor area transferred to the grammar school — it can be linked with the early poem, 'A Blunt Invasion'. But the title directs our attention to a minor character, the local simpleton, whose fright at a tale about the devil told by an acquaintance precipitates a minor accident that ends the friendship. The conclusion is too neat and does not emerge, compellingly, out of the central psychological drama. The third addition, 'A Seeing Eye', is about observing but is too close to the

Morality — lessons learned from perfect people — ever to grip. Lastly, the British edition's final story, 'Keening', is a chronological sweep through a lifetime in the manner of 'Cocksfoot, Crested Dog's Tail, Sweet Vernal Grass'. Unlike the earlier story, however, it lacks thematic direction. The ending, 82-year-old Mary *keening*, wailing aloud, over her garden bonfire of *the detritus of years*, slips too readily into self-conscious cliché:

> *She is crying aloud for the burden of her body and its solitariness. She laments because her life is to be one of memories, and she weeps for the sorrow and pleasure which had been hers. Her voice is clear and powerful, she does not halt its rising, its desolate falling.*

There is little here of the startling, hallucinatory precision of the conclusion to the earlier story, nor of its piercing, cadenced emotion.

The quality of the additions makes it difficult to consider THE GIRL FROM CARDIGAN as a resonating sequence. A further problem is that the sixteen stories common to both editions are not all wholly successful, for reasons apparent in the title story. In this tale of local-government corruption in a south Wales valley the narrator's mother persuades her councillor cousin to find a job for her son:

> *'. . . What's more, he can keep his mouth shut.'* She offered this with a curious nod of the head.
> *Its effect on Harvey was instant and terrible. He gaped, he turned pale, and, grasping his briefcase firmly under his arm, he shot off into the traffic. 'I'll see what I can do', he wailed, running.*

This unexpected blend of P.G. Wodehouse and Gwyn Thomas is one instance of a style heightened into unvarying extremes that recurs in a number of the stories. It is not always deployed for ostensibly humorous purposes; more often than not it is an idealizing instrument, as in the description of Uncle Wynford in 'A Flight of Geese':

Nobody could listen more intently to tales told many times before, nobody could time an urgent question more subtly, nobody else could invent such marvellous, rich detail. His voice was like an instrument. He could use it to entice, to chill, to bombard . . .

Again, of the grandfather in 'Lurchers':

He was a short, generally smiling man, extravagantly generous. He could whistle like a thrush. He knew where the early flowers grew, the windflower and the primrose, and where the mistle thrush, first of birds to nest, kept her spotted eggs. He never seemed to hurry. His speech was slow and quiet.

All is too good to be true; the sense of strain is apparent.

A further aspect of Norris's idealization is his eagerness to celebrate minutely realized natural phenomena, such as birds, blackberries, sheep, and dogs, and manual activities carried out perfectly, such as cleaning football boots, using a snooker cue, playing pitch-and-toss, or building a bookcase. THE GIRL FROM CARDIGAN can seem cloyingly over-full of experts expertly imparting knowledge to receptive disciples, or responding to the craftsman's world with neo-rhapsodic lyricism that sits uneasily in a realist context. For example, in 'A Piece of

Archangel' Oscar the carpenter inherits his grandfather's tools:

> *He left me all his tools, his lovely chisels, thin and glittering, his saws, his huge square old planes, smoothing planes and jack planes. Over a hundred years old they are, beautiful.*

In addition, a point already made about 'Keening', the endings of a few of these stories are achieved through an aesthetically self-conscious and self-referential style. A further example is the final sentence of 'The Wind, the Cold Wind':

> *But we were all crying, we were all bitterly weeping, our cheeks were wet and stinging with the harsh salt of our tears, we were overwhelmed by the recognition of our unique and common knowledge, and we had nowhere to turn for comfort but to ourselves.*

The incantatory slide into the extremities of grand rhetoric (*our unique and common knowledge*) is not a satisfactory account of the effect on the young of a friend's death. Norris, it might be said, on occasion can write too spellbindingly well for his own good.

Such criticism notwithstanding, THE GIRL FROM CARDIGAN is a fascinating volume. Its difference from SLIDING can be pin-pointed by comparing the two opening stories. 'Waxwings' is essentially positive, about childhood happiness, maturing, enlarging the imagination. 'The Girl from Cardigan' is about a boy from a broken home in a south Wales valley who learns profitable lessons from local government's graft and corruption. For, celebratory elements notwithstanding, in places the later volume is more darkly cynical in its concern with lost innocence, with growing-up as prison-house shades close in. In at least four stories, 'In the West Country', 'A Professional Man', 'The Holm Oak', and 'Keening', there is a strong stress on restlessness, rootlessness, the impulsion to change. Above all there is much about death, as in 'The Kingfisher', 'My Uncle's Story', 'The Wind, the Cold Wind', 'A Seeing Eye', 'Reverse for Dennis' and, once again, 'Keening'. Indeed, the artful inconsequentiality of Norris's approach, at its most extreme in, say, the anecdotal 'In the West Country' and 'Lurchers', is invariably deconstructed by the overall impulse towards death, disaster or sadness. Further, because of the nature of the added tales and because this collection generally is so uneven in quality the sequence is not of the first importance. Individual stories dominate; three of these are among Norris's finest.

One is 'Shaving', about a son shaving his bedridden father. It is a good example of how Norris's best work is so successful. For it begins almost casually: Barry, on the edge of adulthood, returning from playing rugby on a spring morning, is conscious of his physical development and his transformation from being *a small unimportant boy*, and chats in the High Street with a friend and a girl. The emphasis on burgeoning physical strength, on his prowess as a rugby player, on being outdoors in April in the fecund spring of his own life, in this superbly constructed tale contrasts with his bedridden father's debility, wasted physique and exhaustion, and with the *infinite and meticulous care* he takes over shaving him.

The shaving itself is described in great detail, the

ritualistic quality dramatizing Barry's loving concern. Recurring imagery deepens the poignancy:

[Barry] washed his hands as carefully as a surgeon ... he washed [the cup] ferociously, until it was clinically clean ... He was discovering under his hands the clear bones of the face and head.

The surgical analogy is sadly ironic: Barry does not save his father's life; rather, his father becomes aware that family life will be sustained after his death. Barry is a healer only insofar as he enables his father to be tranquil. Most moving of all is the reversal of roles, the father's helplessness in the hands of his son, the necessary transference of power between generations, Barry maturing through the experience. To a great extent the story has an inspirational quality. But it ends with Barry at the open bathroom window, *full in the beam of the dying sunlight ... illuminated in its golden warmth for a whole minute, knowing it would soon be gone.* It ends, that is to say, with a sense of Barry's own helplessness, faced with reminders of death and of time's constant pressure.

'Reverse for Dennis' is about an enviably gifted, red-haired schoolboy whose early promise comes to nothing. He makes a girl pregnant and commits suicide. What makes this more than a slightly dated tale of provincial failure is Norris's handling of the narrator. As Dennis lives through his short, troubled, unsuccessful life, the narrator *was busy with [his] own affairs, growing older, learning to be cool and fashionable, to be amused at everything.* He views life with aesthetic solipsism, regarding others as attractive adjuncts to himself. His reaction to news

of the suicide is typical. *'He had a lot of style,'* I said at
last. *'Dennis would have done it with style. It would
have been a superb gesture.'* His listening friend,
appalled and angry at this response, offers
harrowing details of how Dennis was found. *'When
they carried him out'*, he ends, *'I saw his hair had turned
dark.'* The narrator comments: *It was the detail of the
hair that got me.* His aesthetically indulgent vision is
shattered; Dennis's death matures him.

'Sing it Again, Wordsworth' begins, in the night,
with a despairing narrator. *It seemed to me that I had
no roots, that there was no place, however distant, to
which I could turn at so desolate a moment.* Lying awake
in his own house, set in a garden he has created, he
is *lost*, unable even *to imagine the feel of the spade in
my hand.* As for the images of his childhood, *I
have travelled away from those places for half a lifetime.
Their summers are thin and cold, their voices inaudible.*
The sustaining context — familiar surroundings
in a natural world, the remembered past, those
Wordsworthian touchstones — no longer seem to
count.

Reminiscences of beautiful places in which the
narrator had stayed or lived develop the opening
ideas. For, despite the ravishing natural beauty of
Dysynni, or Dorset, or Seattle, or County Cork, the
narrator realizes he has always remained *an outsider
and an alien* with, consequently, an *insatiable thirst
for other places. I cannot remain at peace for long in one
place.* The first part of the story ends with the
narrator driving through a rainy night, getting lost
during a journey from north Wales to his home in
southern England. Seeing a river, he stops in the
darkness to discover he is in front of the abbey at

Tintern. *A miracle of the night had brought me there,* down unknown roads, to a familiar, experienced place with comforting connotations; *I danced a little soft-shoe shuffle at the side of the road, in honour of William Wordsworth,* suddenly at ease with himself and his world.

The second part of the story describes the narrator's college friendship with Arthur Marshalsea. The names, from LITTLE DORRIT, are reminders of the trapped, helpless hero, Arthur Clennam, and the Marshalsea Prison that symbolizes the social and psychological restrictions that dominate that novel. Yet, Arthur Marshalsea is idealized through rosy memory as the epitome of youthful energy, vigour and fun, as a superb sportsman, the life and soul of all encounters and, since these memories are wholly devoid of girls and sexual tension, the supreme man's man. After happy college days they meet at Arthur's wedding before the friendship fades as time passes. Many years later, on impulse, when about to visit Birmingham and knowing Arthur to be living in that area, the narrator makes arrangements to meet him again. The daughter phones: a brain virus has made her father helpless and she warns the narrator of what he will find.

The story's final part returns us to the beginning: the shocked narrator waking lost and distressed. What will he say to the broken man? Certainly he cannot reminisce. Rather, he will talk of his own experiences of beautiful places, of Dysynni, Seattle, *his dark, unintentional journey to Tintern*:

But all the time I'm thinking of Arthur lying nine weeks in a coma ... Where was he then? He must have been away

somewhere in some solitary darkness, weightless, without
senses. I imagine him moving on some dark beach, so
lightly he does not disturb a grain of the sand. He can feel
nothing. I should like to know where he was then; I am
consumed with a curious pity for Arthur Marshalsea, his
useless legs, his halting speech. I see in him a terrible
general fate about which we shall know very little. The still,
sad music of humanity . . . wasn't it? Sing it again,
Wordsworth.

In Arthur's fate we see the appropriateness of his
name: like Clennam he is imprisoned in mind
and body. But Norris's is the bleaker vision:
whereas Clennam's fate proceeded from mainly
understandable personal and social circum-
stances, Arthur's is the result of an arbitrary,
undeserved, unexpected disaster explainable
only in terms of the immediate physiological
condition. In altering the narrator's idea of his
friend it destroys his sense of his own past and of
a present that included sustaining, as distinct
from bitterly ironic, memories. Arthur Marshal-
sea's fate overwhelms even the most attractive of
those memories, whether of college days, places
of breathtaking natural beauty or moments of
contextual harmony. LITTLE DORRIT overwhelms
Wordsworth, such intertextuality giving Norris's
story a relevance far beyond the personal. The
narrator is made to accept that his own and
everyone's likely fate is complete disorientation,
wandering alone in darkness, having lost the
power to feel. Once again, here is a terrifying
glimpse of a wholly secular conception of death.
The narrative stance — gazing out of one world
into another — is characteristic, but what is now
seen is at the opposite extreme from the vibrant,

beckoning, creative world once found, almost daily, in a Merthyr bookshop.

The final two sentences of the story return us to Wordsworth and, by implication, to the concern of 'Tintern Abbey' with roots and orientation. But the flippancy of the close and, in recalling student harmonizing once led by an Arthur who now cannot sing at all, its poignant irony, marginalize such consoling ideas. Rather, the seeming subversion of the almost unbearable emotional tension of this conclusion is, paradoxically, a last reminder of the inescapable bleakness of our common end.

V

Leslie Norris's reputation is firmly based on his poetry and short fiction. But, though he has never become a 'man of letters' in the wide-ranging manner of his friend Glyn Jones, he has other literary achievements to his credit and these must now be described briefly.

For some years he has written poems for children, many of which have been broadcast in BBC radio programmes for schools. *I had to learn to look at the world with newer eyes*, he writes, *and to be perfectly clear in what I said.* Such writing is distinguished by skilful rhythmic and rhyming effects, by humour and, at times, by an element of attractive wish-fulfilment: the boy who scores the perfect goal, for example, or is given a pet on which he had set his heart. Very occasionally a more serious note is sounded, as in 'A Man in Our Village' when, even though a dog saves his master's life,

> He sold her, although she had saved his life.
> Would you have done that, would you?
> I don't think anyone could have done that.

Notable for its imaginative ingenuity and charm is a series of poems about the Nativity, included in NORRIS'S ARK, which treats the event from the point of view of animals: the camels, the stable-cat, the mice, the shepherd's dog and the cattle. All in all, his poems for children allow him to indulge his anthropomorphic tendencies. The result is invariably delight.

As an occasional reviewer for POETRY WALES, THE ANGLO-WELSH REVIEW and THE NEW WELSH REVIEW, mainly on books by and about Welsh authors, he has written sound, commonsensical pieces that tend to praise qualities his own works possess. Thus Vernon Watkins is commended for his use of detail, George Ewart Evans for his capacity to observe, Raymond Garlick for his craftsmanship, Jeremy Hooker for his visual qualities. In an interesting review of CROW Ted Hughes is praised for his *complete observation* and, perhaps arguably, his celebratory quality. But Norris can be critical, as, for example, in his review of Dora Polk's VERNON WATKINS AND THE SPRING OF VISION: her reading was not always up-to-date, he observed, her scholarship not always convincing. And, elsewhere, since he proceeds from a regard for the *orderly, quiet voice, the voice of true speech,* as he wrote of Edward Thomas, he finds Movement poets *cautious and pedantic,* New Romantics *wild and meaningless.*

This willingness to speak his mind characterizes his more sustained literary criticism, such as his essays on Edward Thomas and Vernon Watkins. Thus he is sharply critical of clumsy inversions in the former's 'A Long Small Room' and considers the latter's 'Autumn Song' to be *a weak little poem.* Surprisingly, given his general admiration for Edward Thomas, he considers him overpraised as a nature poet because, unlike John Clare or Andrew Young, *when he is explicitly observant, he is . . . not really communicating more than bare information.* Even in his affectionate monograph on Glyn Jones he

finds structural faults in his friend's fiction and
some poems too overloaded with description.

Norris's critical writing, his reviewing in particular,
looks back to an older *belles-lettres* tradition and not
at all to modern, theorized literary criticism. And
even though it is occasionally prone to foggy clichés,
in such words and phrases as *vivid* and *lovely* or
infinitely sensitive forthrightness and massive honesty,
it is well able to convey genuine pleasure in what he
likes to read.

A well-researched and perceptively introduced
edition of Lady Charlotte Guest's translation of THE
MABINOGION, sensitive editing of two volumes
commemorating, respectively, Vernon Watkins and
Andrew Young, and a moving, dramatized history
of Merthyr entitled VOICES OF THE PLACE, broadcast
in 1973, are among the more important of his other
occasional tasks.

From RANSOMS onwards he has published trans-
lations. Initially these have been of poems in Welsh,
even though he is not fluent in the language. He
wrote, facetiously, of his attempt at Gruffydd
Grug's 'The Yew Tree', that he used *David Bell's
version, Conran's version, some inspired guessing by
Kitty, plus some confusing information from* Y
Geiriadur Mawr. His main interest has been in
Dafydd ap Gwilym. He will never be the scholars'
choice: he tends to ignore textual problems, such
as the doubtful status of part of 'The Fox', or the
well-known crux of *Cypris* in 'The Seagull'.
Occasionally he is simply too modern and too free,
as in 'The Girls of Llanbadarn':

> *'Is he like that? Then no chance',*
> *Says the friend, with a cold glance,*

compared with Bromwich's authoritative version:

> *'Is that how it is with him?'*
> *the other by her side replies.*

Bromwich is accurate but awkward. Norris preserves rhyme; his version certainly reads more like a poem. But *Then no chance* is hardly a medieval colloquialism. Elsewhere his attempt to preserve as much as possible of what is usually lost in translation occasionally works well, despite scholarly negligence, as in lines from 'The Seagull':

> *Copper-curled, curved as Venus,*
> *How beautiful the girl is.*
> *O seagull, but see her face,*
> *Loveliest on the world's surface,*
> *Then bring me her sweet greeting,*
> *Or my certain death you bring.*

Compare Conran, who knows no one really knows what *Cypris* means, who is far more of a poet than Bromwich but does not always avoid syntactical awkwardness:

> *Cypris courted 'neath copper,*
> *Loveliness too perfect-fair.*
>
> *Seagull, if that cheek you see,*
> *Christendom's purest beauty,*
> *Bring to me back fair welcome*
> *Or that girl must be my doom.*

In the lyrical intensity of Norris's lines we can reach across the years to realized love. His ap Gwilym here comes alive in our time.

The same reservations about accuracy apply to the translations of Gwenallt's two great poems, 'Rhydcymerau' and 'The Dead'. Norris's version of the former has its powerful moments, for example, in the final line. His rendering, *And the torrent of rain washes them, they are dried by the rubbing wind,* is more powerful than Clancy's — *And washed by the rain and dried by the wind* — and comparable with Conran's: *And the rain washes them, and the winds lick them dry.* But, here again, he has preferred the poetic to the accurate. 'The Dead', however, defeats him comprehensively. The grandeur and rhetorical power of Gwenallt's words reach beyond individual deaths to evoke those of a community and a nation; they simply cannot be handled in a style close to the conversational. When one of Gwenallt's greatest lines, translated by both Clancy and Conran as *silicotic roses and lilies pale as gas,* describing the flowers placed on the graves of those killed by inhuman industrial exploitation, is translated as *gasping roses/And lilies pale as ice,* we realize, sadly, that even such a fine poet/translator as Norris finds 'The Dead' beyond him.

In 1989 he and Alan Keele, a professor of German at Brigham Young University, published a translation of Rilke's THE SONNETS TO ORPHEUS. Their aim is *to offer the reader as near an experience of the poem as possible.* Norris has no German so Keele provided literal translations, possible alternatives, and suggestions about difficulties; Norris *turned his material into verse form.* The results, as with his best translations from Welsh, are always interesting and at times deeply impressive. A comparison of Norris's version of the opening lines of Sonnet I, 7, with a well-known modern translation is revealing. Norris translates:

> *Praising, that's it! He was designed to praise,*
> *and came like rich ore from the silent mine.*
> *He came, oh, with his heart a mortal press*
> *for humankind of an immortal wine.*
>
> *Nor does his voice dry in a dusty gape.*

C.F. MacIntyre's reads:

> *Praising, that's it! One ordained to praise,*
> *he sprang like ore from the silence of stone.*
> *His heart, oh, perishable winepress*
> *of an infinite wine, for man alone.*
>
> *His voice no dust can choke or dim . . .*

Setting aside questions of accuracy, Norris's preference for the concrete image, such as the *silent mine* and the *dusty gape*, his sustained mellifluousness and avoidance of stiltedly 'poetical' diction, makes his version the powerful aesthetic experience that MacIntyre's is manifestly not. Again, in Sonnet II, 22, Norris's ninth line, *Today's abundances are flashing by*, is far more poetically sensitive than the unfortunate balance-of-payments connotations of MacIntyre's *Today the same surpluses rush past.*

The Norris/Keele translation of THE SONNETS TO ORPHEUS reads like poetry. Further, it reveals Norris's deep empathetic relationship with Rilke's

work. This is, perhaps, not surprising, for Rilke's
concern with time passing, with the poet's ability to
retrieve something of what has been lost, and, in
the Orpheus sequence, with the juxtaposing of two
separate worlds, in this instance the real and the
underworld, would have struck responsive chords
in this modern Welsh poet of memory and glimpsed
alternatives.

We are reminded, once again and finally, of the boy
in the bookshop who became and has remained the
poetic borderer looking out, the outsider looking
in. We are also reminded of the even younger boy
in Brinley Phillips's classroom staring intently
through a hole in cardboard, for his gaze, his
thematic range, has become more and more
concentrated, his style, in his poetry certainly,
sparer, more controlled and, perhaps paradoxically,
more intense. Because of this, because he has car-
ried the effects of his formative years into a career
sustained outside Wales, because of his dem-
onstrable affinity with writers such as Wordsworth,
Edward Thomas and Andrew Young who have,
despite their varying backgrounds, worked within
the mainstream of English literature, Norris extends
our sense of what it is to be a Welsh writer.

And because he has always been a dedicated
craftsman, working assiduously to re-enact
experience in words, the work of his maturity, even
that which, occasionally, is flawed in structure or
intent, invariably has moments of aesthetic delight.
The high points of his career, such as the poems,
'Water', 'A Glass Window', 'Lear at Fifty' and the
superb late sequences, the volume SLIDING and such
individual stories as 'Sliding', 'Three Shots for

Charlie Betson' and 'Sing it Again, Wordsworth', are among the finest achievements of modern Welsh writing. In these works, as in so many others, increasingly so in the work of recent years, that capacity to delight is accompanied by a capacity to disturb through a vision essentially pessimistic, sometimes despairing and becoming at times in his later poetry and prose bleakly secular. For Leslie Norris, in his work as in his life, has never been predictable. Even as he moves into his seventies he retains the ability to surprise. We are fortunate that his own line from 'Bridges' — *launched, hovering, wondering where to land* — can still describe his distinguished and, happily, unfinished literary career.

Bibliography

LESLIE NORRIS

Manuscripts

University of Durham Library
Letters to William Plomer.
University of Exeter Library
Letter to Charles Causley.
The John Rylands University Library of Manchester
Letters to Richard Church.
Leeds University, Brotherton Library
Letters to Alan Ross.
National Library of Wales
Planet Archive, *passim.*
Poetry Wales Archive, *passim.*
Welsh Arts Council Correspondence File (MS of 'Voices of the Place').
MS 19754E (letter to Harri Webb).
MS 21711E (letter to Elwyn Davies).
Reading University Library
Chatto & Windus Archive 1966-1974.

Poetry

TONGUE OF BEAUTY, London, The Favil Press, 1943 (Resurgam Younger Poets, 9).

POEMS, London, Falcon Press, 1946 (Resurgam Books).

98   THE LOUD WINTER, Cardiff, The Triskel Press, 1967.

FINDING GOLD, London, Chatto & Windus and The Hogarth Press, 1967 (The Phoenix Living Poets).

RANSOMS, London, Chatto & Windus and The Hogarth Press, 1970 (The Phoenix Living Poets).

MOUNTAINS POLECATS PHEASANTS and Other Elegies, London, Chatto & Windus and The Hogarth Press, 1974 (The Phoenix Living Poets).

WATER VOICES, London, Chatto & Windus and The Hogarth Press, 1980 (The Phoenix Living Poets).

WALKING THE WHITE FIELDS: POEMS 1967-1980, Boston, Mass., Little, Brown, 1980 (An Atlantic Monthly Press Book).

SELECTED POEMS, Bridgend, Poetry Wales Press, 1986.

SEQUENCES, Layton, Utah, Gibbs M. Smith, 1988 (Peregrine Smith Books).

A SEA IN THE DESERT, Bridgend, Seren Books, 1989.

Poetry: special/limited editions

'The Ballad of Billy Rose', Leeds, Northern House, 1964.

'Curlew', St Brelade, Jersey, Armstrong, 1969.

'His Last Autumn', Rushden, Sceptre Press, 1972.

'Stone and Fern', Winchester, Southern Arts Association, 1973.

'At the Publishers', Berkhamsted, Priapus Press, 1976.

ISLANDS OFF MAINE, Cranberry Isles, Maine, Tidal Press, 1977. With monotypes by Charles E. Wadsworth.

'Ravenna Bridge', Knotting, Sceptre Press, 1977.

'Hyperion', Knotting, Sceptre Press, 1979.

A TREE SEQUENCE, Seattle, Sea Pen Press & Paper Mill, 1984. With wood engravings by Gretchen Daiber.

——, another edition, Seattle, Spring Valley Press, 1984.

'Ransoms', Newtown, Gwasg Gregynog, 1988. With wood engravings by Anne Jope.

THE HAWK'S EYE, Rexburg, Idaho, The Honeybrook Press, 1988.

Poetry for children

MERLIN AND THE SNAKE'S EGG, New York, Viking Press, 1978. With illustrations by Ted Lewin.

NORRIS'S ARK, Portsmouth, New Hampshire, The Tidal Press, 1988. With illustrations by John Elwyn.

Rainer Maria Rilke, THE SONNETS TO ORPHEUS, trans. Leslie Norris and Alan Keele, Columbia, SC, Camden House, 1989 (Studies in German Literature, Linguistics and Culture 42).

Short stories

SLIDING, New York, Scribner, 1976; London, Dent, 1978.

——, another edition, ed. Geoffrey Halson, London, Longman, 1981. With photographs by Jessie Ann Matthew. Includes eight poems by Norris.

THE GIRL FROM CARDIGAN, Layton, Utah, Gibbs M. Smith, 1988.

——, another edition, Bridgend, Seren Books, 1988. Includes four more stories.

Edition

THE MABINOGION, translated Lady Charlotte Guest, ed. and introduced by Leslie Norris, London, Folio Society, 1980. With wood engravings by Joan Freeman.

Compilations

VERNON WATKINS 1906-1967, edited Leslie Norris, London, Faber, 1970.

ANDREW YOUNG: REMEMBRANCE AND HOMAGE, compiled and introduced by Leslie Norris, Cranberry

Isles, Maine, The Tidal Press, 1978. With mono-types and wood-engravings by Charles E. Wadsworth.

Selected criticism by Leslie Norris

'The Poetry of Vernon Watkins', POETRY WALES, 2, Winter 1966, 3-10.

'The Poetry of Edward Thomas', TRISKEL ONE, ed. Sam Adams and Gwilym Rees Hughes, Swansea and Llandybïe, Christopher Davies, 1971, pp. 164-78.

'Seeing Eternity: Vernon Watkins and the Poet's Task', TRISKEL TWO, ed. Sam Adams and Gwilym Rees Hughes, Llandybïe, Christopher Davies, 1973, pp. 88-110.

GLYN JONES, Cardiff, University of Wales Press, 1973 (Writers of Wales).

'A Land Without a Name', POETRY WALES, 13, Spring 1978, 89-101. On Edward Thomas.

'A Profound Simplicity: the Poetry of Andrew Young', NEW CRITERION, 4, 1985, 41-4.

Miscellaneous

Letter in POETRY WALES, 7, 1971, 15-19. Auto-biographical.

POETS OF WALES: DANNIE ABSE, LESLIE NORRIS, Argo Gramophone Record, PLP1155, 1971. Reading their own poetry.

102 Letter in Poetry Wales, 7, 1972, 118-21. On R.S. Thomas.

'The Sense of the Actual: A Conversation with Leslie Norris', Literature and Belief, 3, 1983, 41-53. Interviewed by Bruce W. Jorgensen.

'To Explain the Inexplicable', Poetry Wales, 25, 1989, 42-4. On his approach to writing.

Criticism of Leslie Norris

Walker, Ted, 'On the Poetry of Leslie Norris', Priapus, 11/12, 1967-8, 7-12.

Adams, Sam, 'The Poetry of Leslie Norris', Poetry Wales, 7, 1971, 14-27.

Jenkins, Randal, 'The Poetry of Leslie Norris — An Interim Assessment', Anglo-Welsh Review, 20, 1971-2, 26-36.

Jones, Glyn, 'Leslie Norris', Contemporary Poets, ed. James Vinson, second edn., London, St James Press, 1975, pp. 1122-3.

Smith, David, 'Confronting the Minotaur: Politics and Poetry in Twentieth-Century Wales', Poetry Wales, 15, 1979, 4-23.

Jones, Glyn and Rowlands, John, Profiles, Llandysul, Gomer Press, 1980, pp. 329-31.

Emery, Thomas, 'Leslie Norris', Poets of Great Britain and Ireland, ed. Vincent B. Sherry, Jr., Detroit, Gale, 1984, pp. 264-9.

Jenkins, Mike, 'The Inner Exile: the Merthyr Poems of Leslie Norris', POETRY WALES, 21, 1986, 76-82.

Jones, Glyn, 'A Letter from Glyn Jones', POETRY WALES, 21, 1986, 73-5.

Minhinnick, Robert, 'Leslie Norris — Insistent Elegist', POETRY WALES, 21, 1986, 83-6.

Simpson, Mercer, 'Leslie Norris: Reluctant Exile, Discovered Alien', POETRY WALES, 21, 1986, 87-94.

Baker, Simon C., '"Keeping Short Boundaries Holy": A Study of the Short Stories of Leslie Norris', University College of Swansea, unpublished MA Dissertation, 1987.

Curtis, Tony, HOW TO STUDY MODERN POETRY, London, Macmillan, 1990, pp. 123-9.

LESLIE NORRIS, BBC Wales film, televised 1970, narrated and produced by John Ormond, Cardiff, BBC Wales Library.

ANGLO-WELSH POETS: LESLIE NORRIS, Mold, Clwyd Centre for Educational Technology, 1978. Teaching pack.

Acknowledgements

I am very grateful to Leslie Norris for his friendly patience in answering queries and for his permission to quote from his published and unpublished writings, and to Meic Stephens and Brinley Jones for commissioning this study. For invaluable help of various kinds I am indebted to the following: Simon Baker, Mick Felton, John Harris, Eric Norris, M. Wynn Thomas, Dafydd Wyn. Special thanks are due to John Hubert Davies, former French master at Cyfarthfa Castle School, for showing me around Merthyr, and to Ceinwen Jones of the University of Wales Press. Needless to say, any errors and all opinions contained in this book remain my responsibility.

I am also grateful to the following for permission to use manuscript material: Chatto & Windus (their Archive at the University of Reading); Durham University Library (William Plomer Collection); The National Library of Wales.

The Author

JAMES A. DAVIES was born in Llandeilo, Dyfed, but brought up in Tonyrefail, Tonypandy and, particularly, Pontypool. He was educated at Tonypandy Grammar School, Jones' West Monmouth School and the University College of Swansea. He has a First Class Honours degree in English and a University of Wales Ph.D.

Dr Davies has published JOHN FORSTER: A LITERARY LIFE (1983), DYLAN THOMAS'S PLACES (1988), THE TEXTUAL LIFE OF DICKENS'S CHARACTERS (1989), numerous articles and reviews on Victorian literature and Anglo-Welsh literature, and has edited THE VIEW FROM ROW G (1990), a volume of plays by Dannie Abse.

A former Chief Examiner of Advanced Level English for the WJEC he has also been a visiting professor at Baylor University in Texas. He is a founder member of the University of Wales Association for the Study of Welsh Writing in English and a member of the Welsh Academy. Married, with two children, he lives in Swansea, where he is a Senior Lecturer in the Department of English at the University College.

Designed by Jeff Clements
Typesetting by BP Integraphics, Bath, in
Palatino 11pt on 13pt and printed in Great Britain by
Qualitex Printing Limited, Cardiff, 1991.

© University of Wales, 1991

British Library Cataloguing in Publication Data

Davies, James A.
   Leslie Norris. (Writers of Wales ISSN 0141–5050)
   1. English poetry
   I. Title   II. Series
   821.914

   ISBN 0–7083–1117–2